MONROEVILLE PUBLIC LIBRARY

W9-CED-072

Sports Fundamentals Series

TENNIS
Fundamentals

Carol Matsuzaki
Massachusetts Institute of Technology

Human Kinetics

MONROEVILLE PUBLIC
/JUN 09 2008
LIBRARY

Library of Congress Cataloging-in-Publication Data

Human Kinetics Publishers.
Tennis fundamentals/Human Kinetics with Carol Matsuzaki
    p. cm. -- (Sports fundamentals series)
  ISBN 0-7360-5151-1 (Soft cover)
  1. Tennis. I. Series.
  GV995.T4335 2004
  796.342--dc22   2003020233

ISBN-10: 0-7360-5151-1
ISBN-13: 978-0-7360-5151-4

Copyright © 2004 by Human Kinetics, Inc.

All rights reserved. Except for use in a review, the reproduction or utilization of this work in any form or by any electronic, mechanical, or other means, now known or hereafter invented, including xerography, photocopying, and recording, and in any information storage and retrieval system, is forbidden without the written permission of the publisher.

Acquisitions Editor: Dean Miller; **Developmental Editor:** Cynthia McEntire; **Assistant Editors:** Scott Hawkins and Cory Weber; **Copyeditor:** Jennifer Davis; **Proofreader:** Erin Cler; **Graphic Designer:** Robert Reuther; **Graphic Artist:** Kim McFarland; **Art Manager:** Kareema McLendon; **Photo Manager:** Dan Wendt; **Cover Designer:** Keith Blomberg; **Photographer (interior):** Dan Wendt; **Illustrator:** Tim Shedelbower; **Printer:** United Graphics

Human Kinetics books are available at special discounts for bulk purchase. Special editions or book excerpts can also be created to specification. For details, contact the Special Sales Manager at Human Kinetics.

Printed in the United States of America   10 9 8 7 6 5 4

Human Kinetics
Web site: www.HumanKinetics.com

United States: Human Kinetics
P.O. Box 5076
Champaign, IL 61825-5076
800-747-4457
e-mail: humank@hkusa.com

Canada: Human Kinetics
475 Devonshire Road, Unit 100
Windsor, ON N8Y 2L5
800-465-7301 (in Canada only)
e-mail: orders@hkcanada.com

Europe: Human Kinetics
107 Bradford Road
Stanningley
Leeds LS28 6AT, United Kingdom
+44 (0)113 255 5665
e-mail: hk@hkeurope.com

Australia: Human Kinetics
57A Price Avenue
Lower Mitcham, South Australia 5062
08 8372 0999
e-mail: liaw@hkaustralia.com

New Zealand: Human Kinetics
Division of Sports Distributors NZ Ltd.
P.O. Box 300 226 Albany
North Shore City, Auckland
0064 9 448 1207
e-mail: info@humankinetics.co.nz

Welcome to Sports Fundamentals

The Sports Fundamentals Series uses a learn-by-doing approach to teach those who want to play, not just read. Clear, concise instructions and illustrations make it easy to become more proficient in the game or activity, allowing readers to participate quickly and have more fun.

Between the covers, this book contains rock-solid information, precise instructions, and clear photos and illustrations that immerse readers in the sport. Each fundamental chapter is divided into four major sections:

- You Can Do It!: Jump right into the game or activity with a clear explanation of how to perform an essential skill or tactic.
- More to Choose and Use: Find out more about the skill or learn exciting alternatives.
- Take It to the Court: Apply the new skill in a game situation.
- Give It a Go: Use drills and gamelike activities to develop skills by doing and gauge learning and performance with self-tests.

No more sitting on the sidelines! The Sports Fundamentals Series gets you right into the game. Apply the techniques and tactics as they are learned, and have fun—win or lose!

MONROEVILLE PUBLIC LIBRARY
4000 GATEWAY CAMPUS BLVD
MONROEVILLE, PA 15146

WILLIAM H. HOLMES
OREM, UTAH

Contents

Introduction

Tennis is truly a lifetime sport. Once you learn the basic skills, the benefits of playing are endless—fitness, friendly competition, and personal improvement, to name a few. Let's get started!

The goals of this instructional book are to get you started in this wonderful sport and to give you a working knowledge of tennis. It should help you understand the basics of a sport and how to perform these basics. Most of the book will focus on the basic stroke techniques. Variations to those techniques will be presented, as well as drills and games, so that you can take it to the court. Singles and doubles tactics will be covered as well.

Before getting started, it's important for you to familiarize yourself with the playing field and the equipment that you will be using.

Tennis Court

There are several types of playing surfaces for tennis: hardcourt, clay, grass, indoor carpet, and variations of these. Most outdoor tennis courts in the United States are hardcourt. The major difference among the surfaces relative to playing tennis is how the ball bounces. Hardcourts give the truest bounce. Balls tend to skid on grass and some indoor carpet material. On clay, the court absorbs a lot of the bounce, creating a slower game.

All tennis courts have the same dimensions. While most tennis courts have both singles and doubles sidelines marked, some do not have doubles sidelines. This means that only singles may be played on these courts.

Figure 1 illustrates a tennis court with its dimensions and the proper terminology for the lines. Each line has its own name. The net is 42 inches high at the sides and 36 inches at the center. In the center, the net is held down by a center strap.

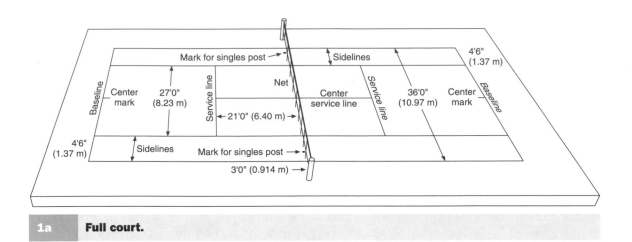

1a Full court.

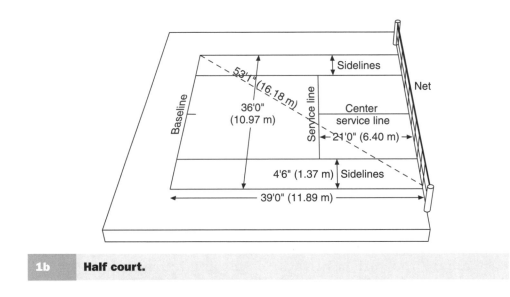

1b Half court.

Tennis Rackets

There are several things to keep in mind when choosing a tennis racket. Remember that if you are getting a racket for the first time, you should not spend too much money on it. As your game improves, you will gravitate toward rackets with characteristics and qualities that match your style of play.

Choosing the right grip size is a very important part of racket selection. Pick a grip that is too small and you will inevitably squeeze the racket handle too tightly. A grip that is too big will result in loss of control.

Grip sizes for tennis rackets are sold in 1/8-inch increments. A good way to figure out what grip size to use is to measure the distance from the middle palm line of your dominant hand to the tip of your ring finger. Most measurements will fall between four and five inches. Another way to select a grip size is to hold the racket in your hand. You should be able to fit at least one finger between the tip of your middle finger and your thumb.

A racket's stiffness or flexibility is determined by the materials used in its construction, its shape, and its thickness. A stiff racket yields a much faster ball off the strings. Because the ball does not stay on the racket very long, it does not lose much velocity. A flexible racket absorbs the ball's velocity, then sends it back. The ball is on the flexible racket for a relatively longer amount of time than on a stiff racket. This allows the player to put more spin on the ball. The bottom line is that a stiff racket generates more power and a flexible racket offers more control. There are many rackets that fall between stiff and flexible.

Many rackets come in midsized and oversized versions. Midsized rackets have a head size of about 95 square inches; oversized rackets have a head size of about 110 square inches. While the two head sizes do not make a huge difference when a ball is struck in the sweet spot, the bigger head will reduce vibration for off-center hits. A larger frame is better for a beginning player.

While the overall weight of a racket has some significance, the balance, or swing weight, of the racket is more important. After all, you are more interested in knowing how the racket behaves in motion, not at rest. Without knowing the actual swing weight, you can determine if a racket is head-heavy or head-light. Head-heavy rackets have a high balance point (center of gravity), kind of like a hammer. These types of rackets offer more power, but less control. Head-light rackets have a lower balance point, offering less power, but easier maneuverability.

The standard length for tennis rackets is 27 inches. Long-body rackets, which are 1/2 to 1 1/2 inches longer, have come out in the past few years. Although this longer length gives extra power, the standard-length rackets are recommended for players who are learning.

Most inexpensive rackets come strung right off the shelf. But what if yours is not strung or you break a string? What type of string should you get? Basically, there are two types of string: synthetic and gut (table 1). Most recreational players use synthetic because it is inexpensive and durable, usually a good bet. Gut provides a better feel for the ball, but it is expensive and fragile.

Table 1

STRINGS		
STRING TYPES		
Synthetic—cheap and durable		Gut—expensive but gives better feel for ball
GAUGES		
15 (thick)	16 (medium)	17 (thin)
TENSIONS		
Tight for control		Loose for power

String gauge is simply the thickness of the string. There are basically three choices: 15, 16, or 17, with 15 being the thickest. Thinner gauge string is livelier, while thicker gauge string is more durable. For beginning players, 15 or 16 gauge string is recommended.

Recommended string tensions vary from racket to racket. Each racket will have a range of recommended tensions listed, usually on the inside of the throat. As a general rule, tighter string tensions give better control and looser string tensions give more power.

Tennis Balls

Two factors that determine what kind of tennis ball you should use are court surface and altitude. Since you most likely will play on hardcourts near sea level, pressurized (in a vacuum-sealed container), extra-duty (they last longer) balls are recommended. Nonpressurized tennis balls are for high altitude play. Regular-duty balls are for softer surfaces such as clay, grass, and some indoor surfaces. Using extra-duty balls on grass will create much faster play than normal. Also, using extra-duty balls on clay will create much slower play than normal.

Tennis Shoes and Attire

As far as shoes go, any shoe that is meant to be worn for a sport that involves forward, backward, and lateral movement should do. Shoes should provide good lateral support and have nonmarking soles. Running shoes are not good for playing tennis. They do not provide good lateral support nor have non-marking soles.

The most important factor for clothing is comfort (figure 2). Wear clothing that doesn't inhibit your movement. Another good idea is to wear shorts, skirts, or sweatpants with pockets that you can put tennis balls in.

Preparing to Play

Stretching is a very important part of getting your body ready for action. Every time you step onto the court, you should engage in your stretching routine. It takes only a few minutes, and if done correctly, should help prevent injury as well as make you stronger.

Stretching should be done in two parts—dynamic and static. Dynamic stretching increases the blood flow to your muscles and gets them ready to be contracted and stretched. Once your muscles are warmed up, they are ready for static stretching. Static stretching increases the range of motion in the muscles so that they are ready to play!

2   **A well-dressed tennis player.**

Dynamic Stretching

Here are some good examples of dynamic stretching that you can do on the tennis court before playing.

LAPS AROUND THE TENNIS COURT

This is a simple yet useful way to get your muscles warmed up. Jog two laps around the perimeter of the tennis court.

THE TRAIN

Start at one intersection of the baseline and doubles sideline facing the net (figure 3). Jog forward to the net, sidestep to the singles sideline, backpedal to the intersection of the singles sideline and the service line, then shuffle to the center service line. At the intersection of the center service line and service line, jog to the net. Backpedal to the service line, then shuffle toward the other singles sideline. At the intersection of the service line and singles sideline, run to the net, then sidestep to the doubles sideline. From there, backpedal all the way down to the baseline. At the baseline, shuffle all the way across to the other doubles sideline. Repeat once more.

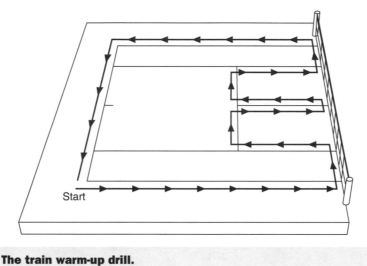

Start

3   **The train warm-up drill.**

HIGH KNEES AND BUTT KICKS

For the high knees, start at the baseline and jog toward the net. Bring your knees up high as though you are bringing them to your chest. Once you reach the net turn around and return to the baseline. Repeat.

For the butt kicks, follow the same jogging procedure as the high knees, but instead kick up your feet behind you and try to get your heels up to your butt.

Static Stretching

After performing dynamic stretches, do some static stretches. Static stretching should be gradual and gentle. It should not be forceful, bouncy, or painful. Hold each stretch for 15 to 20 seconds.

QUADRICEPS STRETCH

You can do this stretch while holding onto something stable if you need to. Raise one foot behind you and grab your shoe. Pull gently. Repeat on the other side.

HAMSTRING STRETCH

Stand with feet slightly apart. Slowly bend over and let your arms hang.

GROIN STRETCH

Stand with feet about two feet apart. Gently lean to one side, flexing your knee on that side. You should feel the stretch in the groin muscle of the straight leg. Repeat on the other side.

CALF STRETCH

Stand about 12 inches from a wall, facing it with your feet together and heels on the ground. Place your hands on the wall, about shoulder-width apart. Gently lean forward against the wall. If necessary, lean farther until you feel the stretch in your calf muscles.

SHOULDER STRETCH

Stand with your right arm outstretched to your right side. Grab an immovable object and gently turn your body to the left. Repeat on the other side.

TRICEPS STRETCH

Drop one arm behind your back, elbow bent. Use your other arm to gently push it down. Repeat with the other arm.

WRIST STRETCH

Extend one arm forward with your palm out, as if gesturing, "Stop." With your other hand, gently pull the fingers back toward you. Repeat on the other hand.

Extend one arm forward with the knuckles facing outward. With your other hand, gently pull the fingers back toward you, under the wrist. Repeat on the other hand.

Rules

To determine service and side for a singles game, one player spins his or her racket while the other player calls it, similar to a coin toss. Once the order of service is determined, the first server starts from his or her right side. The server has two chances to serve the ball into the legal box (the service box diagonal to the one he or she is serving from). If the server misses both serves, it is called a double fault, and the receiver wins the point. If a playable serve is made, then both players hit the ball back and forth until one of the following occurs: a player hits a shot that lands outside of the singles boundary, a player hits a shot into the net, or a player fails to return a legal ball before it has bounced twice. After a point is played, the server alternates service boxes and serves again.

Table 2 is a scoring chart that explains the progression of points in a game.

Table 2

SCORING PROGRESSION

NUMBER OF POINTS	SCORE IN TENNIS TERMS
Zero	Love
One	15
Two	30
Three	40
Four	Game

If the score is tied at 40–40, it is called deuce. A player can win the game only by winning two consecutive points. If the server wins the next point, the point is called "advantage in" (or "ad in" for short). If the receiver wins the next point, the point is called "advantage out" (or "ad out"). At advantage in, if the server wins the next point, the server wins the game. If the receiver wins the point after advantage in, the score goes back to deuce. The opposite is true for advantage out.

The same player serves the entire game. Once a game is finished, the serve goes to the other side. Players should switch ends of the court after every odd game (after the first, third, fifth, and so on). Play should continue until a player wins six games, but he or she must win by a margin of two; this is a set. If the set goes to 5–5, play to 7. If the set goes to 6–6, play a tiebreaker. To play a tiebreaker, the server serves from the right side. After the first point is played, service goes to the other side. In each serving turn that follows, the server gets the opportunity to serve two points, starting from the left. The tiebreaker is played until a player gets to seven points, winning by a margin of two.

A player must win two out of three sets to win the match. Sometimes players elect to play three out of five sets for a match. This is a lot of tennis to play!

In summary, the scoring in tennis goes something like this: A match is composed of sets. A set is composed of games. A game is composed of points. When playing doubles, the only difference is that the alleys are in play. There is no difference in scoring.

Tennis Etiquette

There are a few written and unwritten rules of tennis that you should be aware of when you play.

- Balls that land on the line are considered in. Even if 99 percent of the ball lands out of bounds and 1 percent of it lands inbounds, it is considered in.
- Always call the lines on your side of the court. Do not rely on your opponent or spectators to call your lines. If there's any doubt, it is in.
- Make fair and quick calls.
- Always shake your opponent's hand at the end of a match.
- If one of your balls rolls onto an adjacent court in which a game is in progress, do not run onto that court and get it. Wait until they have finished playing their point, then ask for the ball.
- If you need to cross a court in which a game is in play to get to your court, wait until they are done with their point. Do not cross during a point. This is dangerous and distracting.
- Have fun! Tennis is a great game!

Key to Diagrams

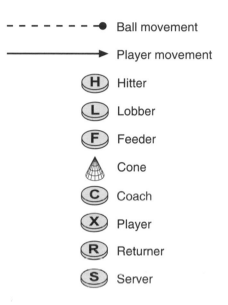

- - - - - - - ● Ball movement

———————▶ Player movement

H Hitter

L Lobber

F Feeder

▲ Cone

C Coach

X Player

R Returner

S Server

CHAPTER

Grips

The grip is the position of the hand on the handle of the racket. Different grips allow you to hit different shots with good body mechanics. Different grips also allow you to hit different shots with varying types and amounts of spin.

The basic grips are the eastern, the continental, the semi-western, and the western. You will see that there is some fluidity among different grips, and you should not be too rigid when using them. As your skills develop, your individual playing style and grip will become unique. There is, however, a correlation between the range of a shot and the grip, contact point, and stance.

This chapter covers the basic grips and their appropriate contact points and stances. Certain advantages and disadvantages go along with each grip. Also discussed are the grips that are inappropriate or ineffective for certain shots.

Eastern Grips

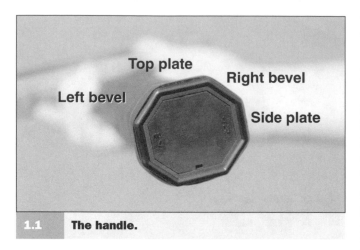

1.1   The handle.

To clarify the hand positions on the racket, figure 1.1 illustrates the different parts of the handle.

The eastern forehand grip (figure 1.2) is a good starting point for a beginning tennis player. It is also appropriately called the shake-hands grip because the hand is placed around the handle as though you were shaking hands with it.

With the face of the racket perpendicular to the ground, the V formed by the thumb and index finger is on the top plate of the handle, with the first knuckle of the index finger on the top right bevel of the handle (for a right-handed player). You also can find this grip by putting the palm of your hitting hand flat on the face of the racket and sliding it down to the handle. The optimal contact point is about hip height and in front of the body. The stance should be closed, which means that for a right-handed player, the left foot should be in front of the right foot.

The eastern forehand is a good grip for the forehand. A beginning player can use this grip to hit backhands, serves, and volleys, though it may be difficult to hit high backhands with this grip. As you get more comfortable with the technique for each stroke, you can slowly change to the continental grip (see page 4) for these strokes. The eastern forehand grip also can be used to hit half volleys in certain situations. Although the

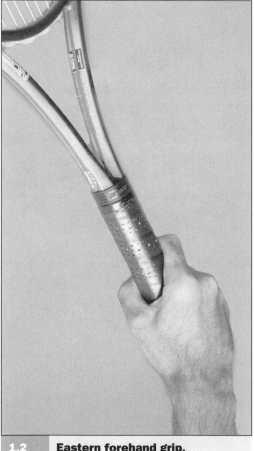

1.2   Eastern forehand grip.

eastern forehand is ineffective for hitting high backhand shots, it is otherwise a good all-around grip. You can hit the ball flat or put topspin on your shots.

The eastern backhand grip (figure 1.3) is a good grip for low or high backhand shots. With the face of the racket perpendicular to the ground, the V formed by the thumb and index finger is on the top left bevel of the handle, and the first knuckle of the index finger is on the center of the top plate of the handle (for a right-handed player). Your index finger should spread slightly up the handle so that the arm and racket feel like one unit. The optimal contact point is at about hip height, or slightly higher, out in front of the body. As with the eastern forehand, the stance should be closed.

The eastern backhand grip is good for putting spin on backhand shots; however, it will make low balls on your backhand side difficult to handle. Advanced players may also choose to use the eastern backhand grip to put additional spin on serves and overhead shots. The half volley can be hit with this grip in certain situations. The eastern backhand grip is ineffective for hitting forehands, however, because it is too wristy.

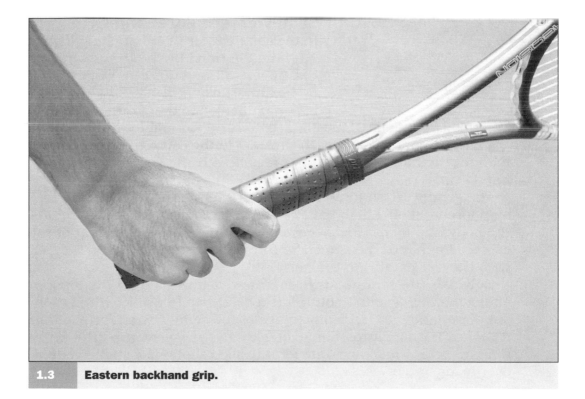

1.3 **Eastern backhand grip.**

1.4　**Continental grip.**

Continental Grip

With the racket on its side, the continental grip (figure 1.4) places the V formed by your thumb and index finger on the top left bevel of the handle. In contrast to the eastern backhand grip, more of the hand is in front of the racket with the continental grip. The index finger spreads slightly up the handle.

The continental grip is a good grip for serves, overhead shots, forehand and backhand slices, and forehand and backhand volleys. This grip is also useful for low forehand and backhand shots and shots that require you to reach wide. The contact point is a bit closer to the body and lower than with eastern grips. The stance should be closed. The continental grip is inappropriate for topspin forehand shots or any shot with a high contact point as it tends to make high shots wristy.

Semi-Western Forehand Grip

In the semi-western forehand grip (figure 1.5), the V formed by the thumb and index finger will be on the top right bevel of the handle when the face of the racket is perpendicular to the ground. The first knuckle of the index finger will be on the side plate of the handle (for a right-handed player). In contrast to the eastern forehand grip, more of the hand is behind the racket with the semi-western forehand grip.

The semi-western forehand grip is used mainly for hitting a topspin forehand off a high ball. The contact point is farther in front of the body and higher (between the waist and chest) than that of the eastern forehand. The stance for the semi-western forehand is open, with the feet parallel to the net.

Because the semi-western forehand allows you to hit topspin shots at a high contact point, it is a good grip to use for hitting topspin forehand lobs. A disadvantage of the semi-western grip is that it makes it difficult to change quickly to the volley grip. The semi-western grip is inappropriate for any slice shots, low shots, volleys, overheads, or serves.

Western Forehand Grip

For the western forehand grip (figure 1.6), the V formed by the thumb and index finger is on the right side plate of the handle when the face of the racket is perpendicular to the ground. For a right-handed player, the first knuckle of the index finger is on the bottom right bevel of the handle.

This grip is not recommended for players who are just learning to play tennis. It is mostly used for hitting forehands with extreme topspin. The contact point is high and in front of the body. The stance is open. It is inappropriate to use this grip for slice shots, low shots, volleys, overhead shots, or serves. The main advantage of this grip is that you can hit a powerful topspin shot off a high ball. This grip can be awkward for beginners because a large part of the hand is in front of the racket rather than behind it.

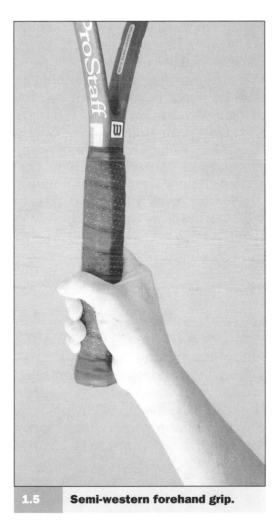

1.5 Semi-western forehand grip.

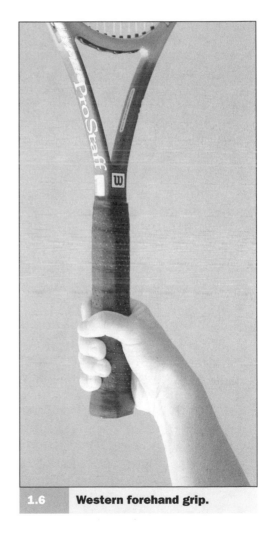

1.6 Western forehand grip.

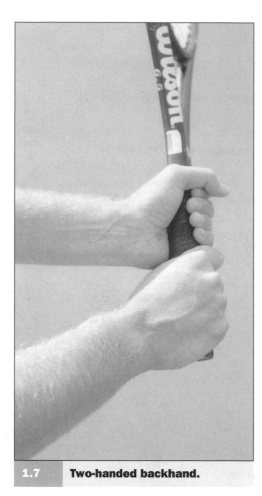

1.7 Two-handed backhand.

Two-Handed Backhand

If you are hitting a two-handed backhand (figure 1.7), use a combination of grips. Place the nondominant hand in the eastern forehand grip. Put the dominant hand in the eastern backhand or continental grip. A right-handed player can think of the two-handed backhand as a left-handed forehand. The contact point is fairly close to the body, in front, at about hip height. Stance should be closed.

The advantages of a two-handed backhand are that the grip allows the player to hit the ball closer to the body and the grip may feel less weak than a one-handed backhand. The disadvantage is that you need to be able to coordinate your right and left shoulders to work together. If you are new to the sport, you should give an honest try to both the two-handed and one-handed backhands to find out which feels more natural. When you select a backhand grip, try to stick with it without changing back and forth. (Exception: always use one hand for a slice backhand.)

Take it to the court

Selecting a Grip

Your nondominant hand plays a key role in switching grips. Use your nondominant hand to support the racket at the throat (or at the grip for a two-handed backhand) so that the dominant hand can relax its hold on the racket. This allows the racket to swivel in the dominant hand. The nondominant hand should turn the racket.

The function of the different plates and bevels of the grip is to give a feeling for the racket head angle without having to actually look at it. With practice you will know which grip and feeling corresponds with which racket head angle.

Because racket head angle is directly influenced by the grip, the grip is a big factor in determining the type and amount of spin you can put on a ball. The eastern forehand and backhand grips hit fairly flat shots. The semi-western forehand can impart topspin. The western forehand will provide a lot of topspin. With the continental grip, you can hit flat or slice shots. With the two-handed backhand, you can hit flat or topspin shots.

Different situations will call for shots with different amounts and types of spin. With practice, you will learn which type of shot is appropriate for the situation. For example, if you need to hit a sharp-angled passing shot, you need to put topspin on the ball so it will go a short distance very quickly and then drop.

Different court surfaces also call for different grips because of the different bounces they produce. Clay courts are the slowest courts. They give a slow, high bounce. Concrete courts produce a medium bounce at a medium pace. On grass courts, the balls will skid on the bounce, producing a fast, low trajectory.

Give it a go

GRIP, CONTACT POINT, SPIN, AND STANCE

Table 1.1 provides a summary of the grips discussed in this chapter and their different characteristics and uses.

Table 1.1

COMPARISON OF GRIPS

GRIP	CONTACT POINT	BALL MOVEMENT	STANCE
Continental	Between knee and hip height, in front of body	Flat or slice	Closed
Eastern forehand	Hip height, more in front of body	Flat or slight topspin	Closed
Semi-western forehand	Between hip and shoulder height, mostly in front of body	Topspin	Open
Western forehand	Between hip and shoulder height, mostly in front of body	Extreme topspin	Open
Eastern backhand	Hip height, more in front of body	Flat or slight topspin	Closed
Two-handed backhand	Hip height, in front of body	Flat or topspin	Closed

GRIP CHANGE

You can perform this drill with a partner. One player holds the racket in the ready position. The other player calls out one of the grips described in this chapter (eastern forehand and backhand, semi-western forehand, western forehand, continental, two-handed backhand). The player holding the racket switches to the grip called without looking down at the racket. Make sure that the nondominant hand holds the racket and turns it to the appropriate grip. Repeat eight times, then switch.

SPIN

This drill can be done alone. It will help you get a feeling for which grips produce which spins and trajectories. Stand at the baseline. Use different grips to hit balls into the other side of the court. Note the differences in spins and trajectories as you change grips.

Set Point

As you practice and gain more experience, the different grips will start to feel more comfortable. Remember that as you evolve and develop as a player, so will the grips that you use. For example, you may start out with an eastern forehand grip to hit your serve, but as you practice and get better, you may find that using the continental or eastern backhand grip gives you more power and control. Or you may find that a certain grip is more efficient in a certain situation.

In the next chapter, we will switch gears from hands to feet. Footwork is a key element in achieving success on the court. Without proper and efficient footwork, it is very difficult to execute strokes correctly.

Footwork

Footwork is very important in executing any stroke in tennis. Being in the right position at the right time makes it possible to hit a shot with the correct technique. If you are not in the right place at the right time, your control or your power will be compromised. Getting to an effective, well-balanced stance at the right position on the court requires a number of footwork techniques.

Most of the footwork techniques used in tennis are fast and quick. That is, the distances you need to cover when you play tennis are not that long (the average distance run for a stroke is two to six yards), but you need to cover them quickly and efficiently. Another important factor is how quickly you can get your body to start moving in a desired direction.

In this section, the ready position and split step are covered, as well as other methods of moving around the court. As you practice these basic court movements, you will find that they play a big part in executing strokes correctly.

Ready Position and Split Step

The ready position and split step are essential to getting a good start to the shot, whether it be a ground stroke, a volley, or an overhead. In every stroke but the serve, the ready position and split step are used in order to "unstick" yourself from the ground and move toward the ball in an efficient manner. A precise split step is especially crucial when time is of the essence, for example, when returning a fast serve or hitting volleys at the net.

The ready position (figure 2.1) is basically an athletic stance that puts your body in a balanced, neutral position so that you can move quickly in any direction. Stand with your knees bent, feet shoulder-width apart or wider, weight on the balls of your feet (imagine someone being able to put a couple of pieces of paper under your heels). Bend slightly at the waist. Keep your shoulders relaxed, eyes looking forward to the other side of the court. Your hands should be on your racket, which should be in front of you at about waist level. Put your dominant hand on the grip. If you hit two-handed backhands, put your nondominant hand on the grip just above your dominant hand. If you hit one-handed backhands, put your nondominant hand at the throat of the racket. You are now in a good ready position!

2.1 **Ready position.**

10

The split step is used to overcome inertia. Inertia is the tendency of matter (you!) to resist changes in velocity (speed or direction). According to Newton's first law of motion, an object with a given velocity maintains that velocity unless acted on by an external force. So, if you are standing on the court in your ready position (velocity equals zero), it will be difficult to make a sudden move to the correct place on the court. You have a lot of inertia to overcome. However, if you add some external force and create some movement just before you know where you need to move, your movements will be a lot quicker and more fluid. This external force is called the split step.

The split step (figure 2.2) is simply a light jump in place from the ready position. The single most important aspect of the split step is its timing. If it is done too early or too late, it is ineffective and/or detrimental to the stroke. Land the split step just as your opponent makes contact with the ball. In other words, the split step is performed in anticipation of your opponent making contact with the ball.

For perfect timing, watch your opponent from the ready position as he or she gets ready to strike the ball. When you think he or she is going to make contact with the ball, execute a light jump, landing back on the balls of your feet. This should get you ready to move in the direction of the ball!

2.2 Split step.

The ready position and split step are crucial to becoming a successful tennis player. Other footwork techniques also are used to get around the court efficiently. This section covers some other forms of footwork used in tennis: the shuffle step, weight transfer step, sprint, and backpedal.

Shuffle Step

The shuffle step (figure 2.3) has many purposes on the tennis court. One of its key uses is to get back to the middle of the court after executing a shot, usually a ground stroke. The shuffle step makes it possible to move back to the middle while facing forward and while ready to change directions.

Start from the ready position. To shuffle to your right, step out laterally with your right foot, then step to your right with your left foot, being careful not to cross your feet. Try to stay on the balls of your feet with your weight slightly forward. Keep your racket in ready

Shuffle Step

| 2.3a | Step to the right with the right foot. | 2.3b | Step to the right with the left foot. |

position. Repeat the shuffle step until you are at the desired place on the court. Try not to bounce too much. Keep your head still and look forward. Your legs and feet do all the moving. This movement is similar to playing defense on a basketball court.

Weight Transfer Step

The weight transfer step (figure 2.4), as its name implies, is used to transfer body weight forward into the shot. This makes it possible to use your whole body to hit the shot rather than just your arm.

Basically, the weight transfer step is executed as you hit a ground stroke. As you take your racket back, all of your weight should be on your back foot. As you accelerate your racket forward to hit the shot, transfer your weight forward. Almost all of your weight should then be on the front foot.

Weight Transfer Step

| 2.4a | As racket goes back, weight is on back foot. | 2.4b | As racket comes forward, weight transfers to front foot. |

Sprint

Sprinting short distances is important on the tennis court. As mentioned earlier, the amount of ground that you need to cover on a tennis court is not overwhelming, but there usually is not much time to cover it.

Sprinting with a tennis racket in your hand and the knowledge that once you get to the ball you need to hit it with the racket complicates things a little. If you are sprinting a short distance to the ball, run with your racket prepared (shoulders slightly turned, racket out; figure 2.5). If you are sprinting a longer distance, for example, the length of the baseline or all the way from behind the baseline to the net, sprint normally until you get close to the ball (figure 2.6). At the beginning of the sprint, pump your arms to accelerate your body. Once you get close to the ball, raise your racket back and execute the shot.

| 2.5 | Sprint with racket ready for short distances. | 2.6 | For long distances, sprint normally until you are close to the ball. |

Backpedal

Backpedaling (figure 2.7) is not used too often on the tennis court. Most backward movements facing forward are done in small increments using a shuffle step. It is, however, a good footwork technique to know. When backpedaling, balance is key.

To backpedal, make sure that you have a clear area behind you. Start out slow, making sure you run on your toes. To help you do this, shift your weight slightly forward. Make sure to use your arms, coordinating them as in running.

2.7 **Backpedaling.**

Starting on the Correct Foot

It is important to use the correct footwork to get in position for a stroke or to execute the stroke. Different game situations call for different types of footwork.

Assume the ready position before each stroke except for the serve. The ready position puts your body in an athletic stance, making you ready to move in any direction. Your body should be in a balanced state in the ready position and both your hands should be on the racket. This lets you change grips if necessary. When changing grips, the nondominant hand should hold the racket while the dominant hand shifts to the appropriate grip.

In the ready position, your head should be relaxed and your eyes should look forward, so you should be able to track the ball. This means that you should be able to visually follow the ball's movement and react with your own movements.

The split step is key to moving toward the ball in a quick, efficient manner. It gets your timing in sync with the ball. It also keeps your feet moving, which is important in overcoming inertia.

The split step also helps you deal with sharp changes of direction. If you land from the split step with most of your weight on your left foot while the rest of your body is leaning to the right, you will find that your body will naturally move to the right. This is important when you need to move in a certain direction very quickly.

The shuffle step is most commonly used in recovery. Recovery happens after you have executed a stroke and need to get back to the middle of the court. The reason the shuffle step is used rather than just running back (even though running is faster than shuffling) is that the shuffle step lets you change directions very quickly. Because your body is facing the other side of the court, you don't have to turn your body all the way around to go the other way.

The shuffle step also is used for moving laterally over short distances, for example, when a ground stroke is only a couple of steps away. Instead of turning and running to the ball, use a shuffle step. The shuffle step will get you there quickly.

The weight transfer step allows you to put your body weight into your shot. Begin with a weight shift to the back foot. As the stroke is executed, shift weight to the front foot. For example, when executing a forehand ground stroke, weight shifts to the back foot as the racket is taken back. As the weight shifts to the front foot, the racket accelerates through the shot.

The most important part of the sprint is the start. You are not going to sprint long distances on the tennis court. The average sprint is only about four yards. Therefore, pushing off from the ground hard and quickly is important. This explosion to the ball is the key factor in an effective sprint.

The backpedal is most commonly used when you are at the net and your opponent hits a slow, high lob. You want to keep the lob in front of you but do not want to hit an overhead shot. This does not happen very often. Nonetheless, the backpedal is a useful technique to practice because it does require quick feet and a lot of balance.

SPLIT STEP—VERBALIZE IT!

This is a partner drill. One person, the feeder, will hit the ball. The other person verbalizes when the split step should occur. Players should stand across the net from one another at the service line, facing each other. The feeder drops a ball in front of himself or herself and hits it (this is called a drop hit). Make sure that the hit is slow and not directly aimed at the player on the other side. The player on the other side begins in ready position and calls, "Hit!" when he or she thinks that the feeder will make contact with the ball. Remember, split steps are anticipatory, not reactionary. Do this 10 times, then switch roles.

SPLIT STEP—DO IT!

This drill uses the same setup as the Split Step—Verbalize It! drill. In this drill, instead of saying, "Hit!" the player should start in a ready position and execute a split step when the feeder hits the ball. Repeat 10 times, then switch roles.

REACTION TOSS

This partner drill works on reaction time. Player A and player B should be about 15 to 20 feet apart. Player B should have his or her back turned to player A. Player A tosses a ball in the air and says, "Go!" This prompts player B to turn around to look for the ball and try to catch it before it bounces twice. This drill emphasizes tracking and hand–eye coordination. Repeat eight times, then switch roles.

As players get better, adjust the tosses (toss lower, farther away, or with spin) to add difficulty.

STAR DRILL

This drill can be done alone or with multiple players or groups. On half a tennis court, put six tennis balls in these positions: the two intersections between the service line and the singles sidelines, the two intersections between the net and the doubles sidelines, the intersection between the center service line and the service line, and the intersection between the center service line and the net (figure 2.8). Put your tennis racket on the center mark.

Start at the center mark. One at a time, sprint to a ball and bring it back to the center mark until all the balls are on the racket. You may have someone time you so that you can improve your speed next time. This drill works on short sprints and changes of direction on the court.

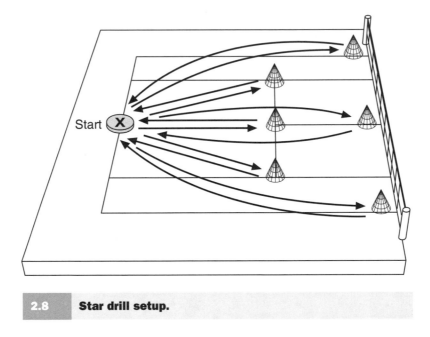

2.8   **Star drill setup.**

A fun variation to this drill is to have teams do this as a relay race. The first player on a team is responsible for bringing the balls in, the second for taking them back out (one at a time), the third player brings them back in, and so on. Have each player go twice. The team to finish first wins the race.

PROGRESSIVE LINE SPRINTS

This drill can be done alone or as a group. You will need two tennis courts (figure 2.9). Line up along the doubles sideline, facing the court. A starter and a timer should be present so that accurate start and finish times can be recorded. When the starter says, "Go!" sprint to the far doubles sideline on the second court. Touch the line with your hand, then sprint back to the original doubles sideline. Touch that line, then sprint to the far singles sideline on the second court, touch the line with your hand, and sprint back to the original doubles sideline and touch the line with your hand. Sprint to the center service line on the second court, touch the line with your hand, and sprint back to the original doubles sideline and touch the line with your hand. Repeat until you've touched all the lines on both courts.

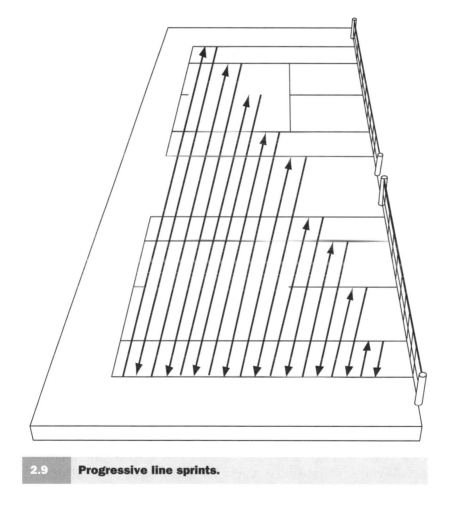

2.9 **Progressive line sprints.**

HEXAGON JUMPS

This drill can be done alone. Using athletic tape on the side of a tennis court, make a hexagon (six sides) with the sides measuring about two feet (figure 2.10). This drill tests your balance, coordination, and jumping skills. Have someone time you. Start inside the hexagon. Without touching a line or missing a jump, jump outside the line and back inside the line. Do this for all sides of the hexagon, going around it three consecutive times.

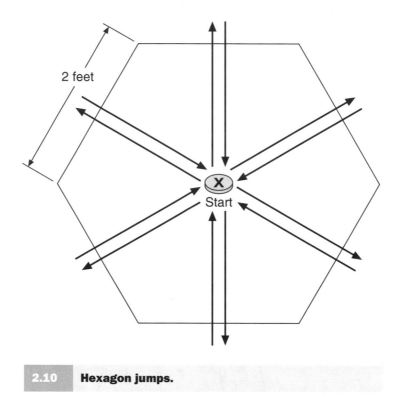

2.10 **Hexagon jumps.**

BALL ROLLS

This drill is done in pairs. It helps you develop good shuffle step technique as well as hand–eye coordination. Player A and player B should be about 10 feet apart, facing each other. Player A should have two balls in hand, with a couple more in a pocket or on the ground. Player A rolls a ball a few feet to player B's right. Player B shuffles toward the ball, retrieves it, and rolls it back. While the ball is rolling back, player A releases the second ball a few feet to player

B's left. Player B shuffles to the left, retrieves the ball, and rolls it back. If a ball goes astray, don't bother chasing it; just put another ball in play. Repeat for 30 seconds and switch roles.

LEADER AND SHADOW

The leader and shadow drill is done in pairs. Decide who will be the leader and who will be the shadow. The leader and the shadow should start about 10 feet apart, facing each other. The leader starts by doing a footwork exercise, such as the shuffle step. The shadow must mirror whatever the leader is doing (figure 2.11). Each footwork exercise should last about three to five seconds. Do this for 30 seconds, then rest for 30 seconds. Switch roles and do the drill for another 30 seconds.

2.11 **Leader and shadow drill.**

Set Point

The more you practice correct, tennis-specific footwork techniques, the more efficient you will be on the court. You will also find that your stroke techniques actually improve as your footwork gets better. You will learn to coordinate your footwork and stroke technique so that your strokes can be fluid and efficient.

Now that you are familiar with the proper grips and footwork, you are ready to learn your first stroke, the forehand!

CHAPTER

Forehand

The forehand is one of the first skills beginners are introduced to. It also is the most frequently hit shot for most beginning and intermediate tennis players.

Simply put, the forehand is a shot that bounces and is hit on a player's dominant side. As a starting point, players should focus on correct technique. It is important to have sound fundamental basics to see steady improvement. The second area of focus should be consistency and control. The last area of focus should be power.

Many types of spin can be put on a forehand—flat, topspin, underspin, or sidespin. There are also differences in stance—open or closed. The backswing may also vary—loop or straight back. The point is, everyone's forehands will look a bit different, but the basic technique should be the same. For example, Venus Williams' forehand is very different from Andre Agassi's forehand, which is very different from Pete Sampras' forehand. Each player has a personalized way of hitting, and each player uses spin as a big weapon in his or her game. We will start with the flat forehand.

Flat Forehand

Many steps are involved in hitting a good flat forehand. Through consistent practice using the correct technique, these steps should develop into a smooth, dependable ground stroke.

Start with the grip. For a flat forehand, use the eastern grip. Next, assume a ready position. Basically, this means that you should be in an athletic stance: feet about shoulder-width apart, weight on the balls of the feet, knees slightly bent, shoulders relaxed, eyes looking straight ahead, racket held with both hands in front of the body (figure 3.1a). Make sure that you are balanced and ready to move.

The next step is the split step (figure 3.1b). As discussed in the previous chapter, the split step occurs just before the ball is hit by the other person in order to overcome inertia and unstick your feet. A split step is done in anticipation, not in reaction, so the movement for the split step should start a moment before your opponent actually makes contact with the ball.

As you land your split step, the backswing starts. Turn the shoulders and open the racket so that the tip of the head of the racket is pointing slightly down and toward the back fence. Turn sideways to the target with the racket still positioned back and low (figure 3.1c).

| 3.1a | Get ready to move. | 3.1b | Perform the split step. |

Your feet should be more than shoulder-width apart to maintain balance. Make sure that your knees are bent.

Next, you must transfer your weight forward as you hit the ball so that your whole body, instead of just your arm, is doing the work (figure 3.1d). With your side to the target, step forward with the left foot if you are right-handed (a left-handed player should step forward with the right foot). This is called the closed stance. Using the correct stance aids in effective transfer of weight.

Contact the ball above the front foot at about waist level, maintaining a firm wrist and a low to high swing. Try to elongate your swing, as if you're hitting five balls lined up right next to each other, instead of just one. As you finish with the follow-through, your racket should end up in front of your body, following the flight of the ball. Make sure to keep your head still and level.

You have just hit the ball, but you are not done! With the racket in the ready position, use the shuffle step to get back to the middle. This is the recovery phase of the shot. Now you are ready to hit another shot!

3.1c   **Execute the backswing.**   **3.1d**   **Hit the ball.**

Although most players have one forehand that is their default forehand, having a variety of forehands to choose from gives you lots of options to resolve various game situations. Slice forehands tend to float and stay low to the ground after the bounce, whereas topspin forehands have a looping trajectory and a kick after the bounce.

Slice Forehand

For a slice forehand, either an eastern or a continental grip may be used. Bring the racket back higher and use a more open racket head angle than you would for a flat forehand (figure 3.2a). Make sure your body is turned and step with your left foot (assuming you are right-handed). Your feet should be more than shoulder-width apart and your knees should be bent. Your racket arm should be slightly bent, the racket face fairly high and nearly vertical.

Start the forward swing by brushing the backside of the ball in a slightly downward direction (figure 3.2b). The bottom edge of the racket should be leading. With practice you should be able to feel that your racket has an open angle. You shouldn't have to look at your racket. Follow through, trying to maintain the same racket head angle. (It may change a bit because of the impact.) At the end of the follow-through, the racket should be even with or above your head.

With practice, you should be able to hit slice forehands that have good net clearance, yet do not go sky-high. If you are finding that

Slice Forehand

| 3.2a | **Backswing.** | 3.2b | **Forward swing.** |

your shots go into the net, try opening up your racket head angle. If your shots are either going straight up or not going very far, try flattening out your shot (closing the racket head angle) a bit more.

Make sure that you maintain control of the shot by hitting it out in front of you. If the ball gets behind you, it is difficult to keep your wrist firm, and therefore your shot will be altered.

Topspin Forehand

For a topspin forehand, use a semi-western or western grip. Take a loopier backswing to aid in imparting topspin (figure 3.3a). This means that you should take the racket back fairly high so that you can loop the racket into the shot. Either the open stance (right foot forward for right-handers, left foot forward for left-handers) or the closed stance may be used. If you are using the open stance, be sure to turn your shoulders and hips. Contact is made higher than with a flat forehand (figure 3.3b). Make sure that the contact point is in front of your body. The follow-through should go over the opposite shoulder, with the wrist breaking at the very end.

An important thing to remember about the topspin forehand is you should try to prolong your stroke for as long as possible. Many

Topspin Forehand

| 3.3a | Backswing. | 3.3b | Forward swing. |

people tend to swing from low to high too quickly. Even though the ball may have a lot of spin, it does not have any depth. If your shots are landing short, slow down your swing speed and concentrate on trying to make the middle part of your swing as long as possible.

Choosing a Forehand

Different situations call for different shots in terms of spin, trajectory, and speed. For example, if you are moving your opponent around the court, it is more advantageous to hit a flat, fast shot instead of a looping, slow one. However, if your opponent is moving you around, it might be better to hit a looping, slow shot to buy some time. Here are some advantages and disadvantages of each of the different types of forehands and some situations that they may be used in.

The advantages of a flat forehand are that the backswing (straight back) is not complicated and the trajectory of the ball is linear and therefore travels through space quickly. This makes it an ideal choice if you want to move your opponent around the court. It doesn't give your opponent a lot of time to recover between shots. The disadvantages of the flat forehand are that the lack of spin makes it difficult to control and the eastern grip makes it difficult to hit high balls.

The advantages of a slice forehand are that contact may be made slightly later (behind the front foot) than with the flat or topspin forehand, the shot is easier to control, the ball will stay low to the ground after the bounce, and the ball will bounce away from the opponent. This makes it an ideal shot for hitting approach shots (the shot hit before attacking the net). The ball tends to stay low after the bounce; therefore your opponent must hit up to you. Another situation in which a slice is used is in the drop shot, which is discussed in detail in chapter 8. The disadvantages of the slice forehand are that the ball may sail out if it is hit with too much racket head speed or the ball may go straight up if the racket face angle is too open.

The advantages of a topspin forehand are that the spin makes the ball drop (which will cut down on length errors), the ball has a kick after the bounce, and the ball travels through space more slowly. (This can be an advantage if you are being moved around and are trying to buy time between shots.) Topspin forehands are useful in maintaining a consistent rally, as the spin gives the ball a looping trajectory. The disadvantages of a topspin forehand are that a bigger backswing is required to hit it, the ball travels through space more slowly (this can be a disadvantage if you are looking to move your opponent around), and you may end up with shallow shots if the hitting zone is not elongated. The semi-western grip makes it difficult to hit balls that are low.

DROP HIT FOREHAND

This drill can be done alone. Stand on the service line, facing sideways, with your nondominant side in front (figure 3.4). Hold the racket in your dominant hand with the racket head directed toward the back fence. Hold a tennis ball in your nondominant hand. Drop the ball in front of you, let it bounce, and hit a flat forehand. (This drill also can be done with slice and topspin forehands.) Try to get at least 7 out of 10 attempts in the opposite court.

3.4 **Drop hit forehand drill.**

SOFT TOSS FOREHAND

This is a partner drill. One player is the feeder, the other is the hitter. Both players stand at the service lines on opposite sides of the court, facing each other. The feeder uses an underhand toss to throw the ball to the hitter's forehand side. The hitter performs a split step on the feeder's release and hits a forehand. Repeat 10 times, then switch roles.

RALLY FOREHAND

This is a partner drill. Partners stand at the service lines on opposite sides of the court, facing each other. The player with the ball starts the drill with a drop hit forehand, hitting the ball to the other player's forehand. Continue the rally, trying to hit the ball to your partner's forehand. Any ball that doesn't bounce twice and is hit as a forehand is legal. Keep count of how many you can hit in a row. Try to get 12 in a row before you attempt the next drill.

FULL COURT CROSSCOURT FOREHAND

This is a more advanced version of the rally drill. Both players should start at the baselines on opposite sides of the court. Again, keep count of how many balls you can keep in play. Remember, any ball that doesn't bounce twice and is hit as a forehand is legal, so HUSTLE!!

Set Point

As you progress, you should see improvements in consistency and control. Don't worry about power yet. Try to get as many balls as you can in the court first. Stick with the basic techniques. Make sure your ready position is good, your weight transfer is effective, and you are swinging from low to high. As you begin to get more consistent with the flat forehand, try incorporating slice and topspin into your forehands.

In the next chapter, you will learn how to hit a backhand, which is a ground stroke on the nondominant side of your body.

Backhand

While some parts of the backhand are the same as the forehand, others are different. Footwork, contact point, weight transfer, and recovery remain the same as the forehand. The things that make a backhand different are the grips and how you coordinate your hands and shoulders.

There are many ways to hit a backhand correctly. Justine Henin-Hardenne hits a one-handed topspin backhand. Steffi Graf used a one-handed slice backhand. Andre Agassi uses a two-handed backhand. The important thing is to be consistent with the backhand that feels most natural to you.

Backhands are a very important part of the game. For example, in a point, if a ball is in the left corner, it would be much more efficient for you to hit a backhand than to run around the ball to hit a forehand.

One-Handed Flat Backhand

To hit a consistent, accurate one-handed flat backhand, it is important to use the continental grip. Using a forehand grip for the one-handed backhand will result in oversupination of the forearm, which can result in tennis elbow. Your nondominant hand should hold the throat of the racket.

The ready position and split step are the same as in the forehand (figure 4.1a and 4.1b). As you land your split step, take the racket back and low using the nondominant hand (figure 4.1c). This also aids in stabilizing the backswing and turning the upper body. Your upper body should be turned sharply, as if showing the back of your shirt to the person on the other side. Have your body weight on your back foot, ready to transfer it forward as you step forward. Make sure your knees are bent.

At this point you should be sideways to the target, as in the forehand. Step forward with your right foot (left foot if you are left-handed).

| 4.1a | Get ready to move. | 4.1b | Execute a split step. |

Your feet should be a bit more than shoulder-width apart. At this point your shoulders should be in line with the direction of the shot. Let go of the racket with your nondominant hand, then lower the racket head so that it can be accelerated forward and upward. Contact should be made in front of the body, and the hitting arm should straighten (figure 4.1d). The racket face should be perpendicular to the ground at the moment of contact. Your nondominant hand should stay behind you in order to maintain balance.

After contact, continue the swing in the direction of the shot. At the end of the follow-through, your racket and side of the body should point toward your shot. Your body weight should have transferred almost completely to the front foot. As with the forehand, make sure that you recover after you have hit the shot. Get in the ready position and use the shuffle step to return to the middle of the court, ready for the next shot.

4.1c   **Bring the racket back.**

4.1d   **Make contact.**

As with the forehand, there are a few ways in which you can hit a backhand. It is recommended that you use either a one-handed or a two-handed backhand, but not both. The exception is the slice backhand. Although slice backhands are almost always hit with one hand, players who use two hands on their flat or topspin backhands use the one-handed slice backhand. The slice backhand is one of the most useful and versatile shots in tennis. It can be used to create situations as well as getting out of a situation by neutralizing the point.

Slice Backhand

For a slice backhand, hold the racket with a continental grip. Your nondominant hand should be at the throat of the racket. As with the one-handed backhand, pull the racket back with your nondominant hand. Instead of pulling it low, pull it fairly high, with the face of the racket head at about shoulder level (figure 4.2a).

The upper body rotation should be much more pronounced than with the forehand slice. Step forward with your right foot (if you are right-handed). Keep your feet more than shoulder-width apart to maintain balance. At the end of the backswing, your racket arm should be bent and the racket face should be very open.

The transition from backswing to forward swing should follow a shallow arc (figure 4.2b). During the stroke, straighten the racket

Slice Backhand

| 4.2a | Backswing. | 4.2b | Forward swing. |

arm. Make contact slightly in front of your body and slightly below chest level. As you contact the ball, transfer your weight to the front foot. Your racket face should remain open as you follow through in the direction of your shot. Your nondominant arm should stay behind you in order to maintain balance.

One-Handed Topspin Backhand

For a one-handed topspin backhand, use a continental or western backhand grip. As with the backhands discussed previously, take the racket back with the nondominant hand (figure 4.3a). Since you will be taking a looping backswing (like with the topspin forehand), take the racket back fairly high. Your upper body should be sharply turned. Step in with your right foot (if you are right-handed).

As you swing the racket forward, let go of it with your nondominant hand (figure 4.3b). Bring the racket below the anticipated contact point so that you can swing in a low to high manner. Make sure you bend your knees to support the upward movement. Straighten the arm just before contact. Contact should be made in front of the body and at about waist level. You should feel like the racket is moving over the ball. This creates topspin.

One-Handed Topspin Backhand

4.3a Backswing. 4.3b Forward swing.

After contact, keep following through with the upward motion. Your nondominant hand should be behind you for balance.

Two-Handed Backhand

To a right-handed player, the two-handed backhand is similar to a left-handed forehand. The left arm should push the racket through the stroke. Often, beginning players tend to try to hit a two-handed backhand mostly with their dominant arm. This results in a lack of coordination between the left and right arms.

From the ready position, place your hands right next to each other on the grip with your dominant hand at the bottom of the grip. Your dominant hand should use the continental grip and your nondominant hand should use an eastern grip. Take a split step, then turn your upper body, taking the racket straight back, keeping both hands on the grip (figure 4.4a). The dominant arm should be nearly straight, while the nondominant arm should be bent. Step forward with your right foot (if you are right-handed).

As you accelerate forward to hit the shot, the head of the racket should be lower than the anticipated contact point so that you swing from low to high (figure 4.4b). Make sure that your nondominant arm

Two-Handed Backhand

| 4.4a | Backswing. | 4.4b | Forward swing. |

and shoulder are pushing the racket forward. This will ensure a smooth stroke. Your feet should be a bit more than shoulder-width apart.

Contact the ball above your front foot and slightly below waist level. At contact, transfer your weight from back to front foot. Both arms should be slightly bent. Continue following through in the direction of the shot.

Selecting a Backhand

As with the forehand, varying the spin, trajectory, and speed of the backhand can come in handy depending on the game situation.

The flat backhand is a useful shot to have when you want to hit a shot away from your opponent.

The slice backhand is one of the most useful shots to know on a tennis court. It is relatively easy to hit, stays low to the ground after the bounce, and can be disguised, allowing you to hit a drop shot off of it. One of the classic uses of the slice backhand is the approach shot. The high backswing of the slice backhand lets you hit the shot when the ball is relatively high, allowing you to hit the ball early. The racket work of the shot allows you to naturally move into the court to a volley position. A shot hit with slice tends to stay low to the ground after the bounce, which makes it difficult for your opponent to return. Your opponent will have to hit up to you.

The one-handed topspin backhand takes some time to develop, but with enough practice, it is a very dependable shot. Because of the spin and trajectory, the ball is likely to land inbounds. Putting topspin on your shot will also make it difficult for your opponent to handle, as the shots will bounce high, therefore pushing your opponent behind the baseline. Another tactical advantage to hitting a topspin shot is that because the trajectory of the ball tends to be very loopy, you can hit extreme angles with less risk of hitting the ball wide.

For beginning players, the two-handed backhand may be a good choice just because there is more stability with the extra hand holding the racket.

DROP HIT BACKHAND

This drill can be done alone. Stand on the service line, facing sideways, with your dominant side in front. Hold the racket in your dominant hand with the racket head directed toward the back fence. Hold a tennis ball in your nondominant hand. Drop the ball in front of you, let it bounce, step in, and hit a backhand. Try to get 7 out of 10 attempts in the opposite court.

SOFT TOSS BACKHAND

This is a partner drill. One player is the feeder, the other is the hitter. Both players stand at the service lines on opposite sides of the court, facing each other. The feeder uses an underhand toss to throw the ball to the hitter's backhand side. The hitter performs a split step on the feeder's release and hits a backhand. Repeat 10 times and then switch roles.

RALLY BACKHAND

This is a partner drill. Both players stand at the service lines on opposite sides of the court, facing each other. The player with the ball starts the drill with a drop hit backhand, hitting it to the other person's backhand. Try to continue the rally, always trying to hit it to your partner's backhand. Any ball that doesn't bounce twice and is hit as a backhand is legal. Keep count of how many you can hit in a row.

CROSSCOURT BACKHAND

This is a more advanced version of the rally drill. Both players start at the baselines on opposite sides of the court. Again, keep count of how many balls you can keep in play. Remember, any ball that doesn't bounce twice and is hit as a backhand is legal, so HUSTLE!! Try to get to 12 consecutive shots.

FIGURE EIGHTS

Now that we know how to hit a forehand as well as a backhand, we can combine the two shots in a drill. This is a partner drill. Players stand at the service lines on opposite sides of the court. One player will be the "down-the-line" player; this player will hit straight shots parallel to the singles sideline. The other player will be the "cross-court" player; this player will hit all shots from his or her deuce side (right side) to his or her partner's ad side (left side) and vice versa (figure 4.5). This should create a figure-eight pattern. After you get to 10 consecutive shots, switch roles and repeat. As you get better, try doing this drill from the baseline.

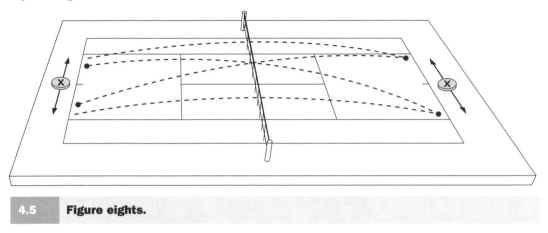

4.5 **Figure eights.**

AROUND THE WORLD

This is a fun group game for six or more people. Line up at the baselines on opposite sides of the net. The coach or feeder puts the first ball into play. Each player hits one shot and runs to the right to join the line on the other side of the court (figure 4.6). If a player hits the ball out of bounds, into the net, or lets it bounce twice, the player gets one out and the ball is dead. A player is out after three outs. The feeder starts the rally after every dead ball. When there are only two players left in the game, instead of running around the court, each player must drop his or her racket and spin around the racket after hitting each shot. The player who remains without getting three outs is the winner.

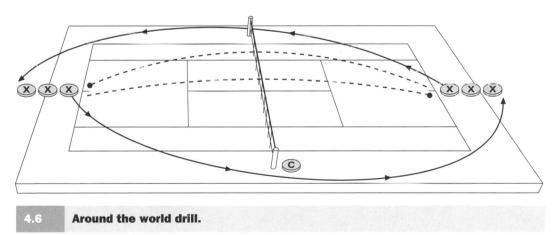

4.6 **Around the world drill.**

Set Point

Now you know how to hit forehands and backhands. It's important to stick with the basics to improve consistency and accuracy. Make sure your ready position, grips, split step, footwork, stroke technique, and recovery are correct.

It takes practice, practice, practice to get used to the different bounces, spins, trajectories, and speeds of the incoming tennis ball. With time and patience, you will be better able to judge where and when you should hit your shots. The next chapter will focus on shots that you hit before they bounce, called volleys.

Volley

The volley is one of the most misunderstood shots in tennis. Most players perceive it as an incredibly difficult shot to hit, probably because there is a lot of emphasis on developing ground strokes when first learning how to play tennis, and also because beginners may fear being at the net. It is actually a simple, uncomplicated shot to execute if done correctly and precisely.

Simply put, a volley is a shot that you hit before the ball bounces. It is usually hit from between midcourt and the net. Most of the work you need to do to hit a consistent, accurate, effective volley is done with your feet, not with your racket, which is a major difference from the ground strokes.

Volleyers such as Martina Navratilova, Stefan Edberg, and Pete Sampras, some of the best in the world, had amazing footwork. They made the racket work look easy by working their feet really hard so that they were always in good position.

Forehand and Backhand Volleys

In general, volleys are hit between midcourt and the net. To practice volleying, stand 8 to 10 feet away from the net in the ready position. Use the continental grip.

For a forehand volley (figure 5.1), start stepping forward with your left foot (if you are right-handed). While keeping the racket head above the racket grip, take the racket back a very short distance on your forehand side. Maintain an open racket face; this means that the racket face should be facing slightly up. The racket face should be above and behind the grip of the racket.

As you start moving your racket forward to hit the volley, step with your left foot and continue moving the racket forward without changing the racket head angle too much. Pretend you are pressing a big button with your racket. If you change the racket head angle, you won't be able to push the button straight on. Your grip should lead the racket head at the beginning of the forward movement.

Contact should be made well in front of your body. Step with your left foot so that your momentum moves forward. As you follow through, the racket will end up in front of your grip. Open up the face of the racket a bit more to put some underspin on the ball. This movement should transition smoothly into the ready position for the next shot.

Forehand Volley

5.1a   Backswing.

5.1b   Make contact.

For a backhand volley (figure 5.2), the ready position and split step are executed the same way as for a forehand volley. As the ball comes to your backhand side, step with your right foot (if you are right-handed). With your nondominant hand at the throat of the racket and your dominant hand at the grip, take the racket back to your backhand side. The racket face should be open, as in the forehand volley. Make sure that the racket face is above and behind the grip of the racket.

As you move forward to hit the volley, release the racket with your nondominant hand. Now this hand will aid in balance throughout the rest of the shot. Keep moving the racket forward, straightening the dominant arm as you follow through. Try to keep the angle of the racket head the same throughout the shot. This open racket head angle will help put underspin on the ball.

Make contact with the ball in front of your body. Step with the right foot (if you're right-handed). This is very important in contributing to the forward movement. Keep following through forward. Your nondominant arm should move farther away from the body in order to maintain balance.

Backhand Volley

| 5.2a | Backswing. | 5.2b | Make contact. |

Use the continental grip for both forehand and backhand volleys. There are two fundamental reasons why there is one grip for both forehand and backhand volleys. First, the continental grip allows for backspin to be imparted on both shots. This backspin allows you to hit deep shots from close up. Second, since you are close to the net, you don't have time to switch grips.

The split step also becomes incredibly important when you hit volleys. As I mentioned, precise footwork is the key to a good volley, and the split step is crucial to getting started. From the ready position, watch your opponent's stroke so that you know when to split step. Have your weight on the balls of your feet. Execute the split step when you think your opponent will hit the ball. As you land, you will know which side of your body you will have to hit the ball on.

Volleys can be hit from almost anywhere on the court. Depending on where you are, you might hit a different type of volley. If you are at midcourt, you might have to hit a half volley. If you are only a couple feet from the net and you are given a floaty ball, you might be able to hit a putaway volley. If you are close to the net and are given a hard shot right at you, you might have to hit a reaction volley.

5.3 The half volley.

Half Volley

A half volley (figure 5.3) is a shot that is hit immediately after the bounce. Technically it is not a volley, but the mechanics of the stroke are very similar to the volley. The half volley is used when the player is standing too close to the point where the ball bounces to hit it as a ground stroke but too far away to hit it as a volley. It is usually hit around the service line but can be hit from other areas of the court as well.

You can use either an eastern or continental grip for the half volley. After executing the split step, take the racket back slightly. Because you will be hitting the ball immediately after the bounce, you must get down low by bending your knees. Widen your stance to maintain your balance from this very low position.

The stroke is a fairly flat swing. Transfer your weight from back to front leg. This is where most of the forward movement will come from. Follow through toward the target. If your contact point is well in front of your body, your stroke will be a fairly long one. If your contact point is close to your body, your stroke will be much shorter. Contact the ball as it rises from the ground. After you execute the shot, keep moving forward toward the net.

Low Volley

A low volley (figure 5.4) can be difficult to handle if the right technique isn't used. The most important thing that a player should do when faced with a low volley is to get down low with the ball!

5.4 **The low volley.**

The low volley is executed in the same way as a volley with a few exceptions: the racket face should be slightly more open in order to aid with net clearance; the body is lowered by bending the knees so that you can put your racket underneath the ball; and your stance should be wider so that you can maintain your balance through the shot in this low position. It's important that you also transfer your weight from back to front leg.

Putaway Volley

The putaway volley is hit from very close to the net. As the term implies, it is used to win the point by putting the ball away and should be the last ball hit in a point. It is important that you hit this volley when the ball is above the net. Find the angle at which you should hit the ball in order to actually put it away off the court.

5.5 The putaway volley.

5.6 The reaction volley.

The putaway volley starts with recognizing that the speed and height of the incoming ball and your position on the court make it possible for you to hit a putaway volley. Once you recognize that you can hit a putaway volley, your next job is to get to the ball before it is below the level of the net. Sometimes it may be a step away, other times you may have to sprint to it.

Once you are close enough to the ball to hit a volley, make sure that you angle your body and racket so that the shot you are about to hit has a sharp angle off the court (figure 5.5). Take your racket slightly back and accelerate forward through the shot. Be sure to keep your feet moving through the point of contact of the volley.

Reaction Volley

Reaction volleys (figure 5.6) are usually hit from very close to the net. Use it when the ball hit to you is fast and aimed right at your body!

Basically, what you need to do now is protect your body. Take the shot as a backhand volley right in front of your body. Taking the shot as a backhand ensures that your own arm won't be in the way of the shot. Make sure that the racket face is perpendicular to the ground and hold on to your racket tightly at the moment of impact. If the racket is not held tightly, it may rotate around in the hand on impact, changing the racket head angle and resulting in a loss of control of the direction of the volley.

Volley Choices

The choice of volley usually depends on your position on the court. For example, half volleys are usually hit from midcourt, while putaway volleys and reaction volleys are usually hit from close to the net. It is important to be aware of your position on the court and to recognize which shot will be most effective.

Half volleys usually are hit when a player is going to the net after hitting a serve or an approach shot. The half volley is the transition shot from a baseline position to a net position. It is a difficult shot but a very useful one. Because the half volley is hit immediately after the bounce, it keeps a player from being forced off the court. It also lets the player rush his or her opponent by reducing the time between the bounce and the hit.

A half volley is also used in situations in which the spin, angle, trajectory, and/or speed of the ball might be tricky. For example, if your opponent hits a very high, deep forehand with a lot of topspin, you might want to hit a half volley from the baseline. Otherwise, if you let it bounce, it might bounce over the back fence before you can even get your racket near it!

Low volleys are also usually hit when a player is going to the net. It is important that you keep the racket face open and keep moving forward to get a good trajectory on the ball.

Putaway volleys are usually hit after you have just hit a very forceful shot to cause a weak response from your opponent. It is important that you hit this volley when the ball is above the height of the net. A possible situation in which you want to use a putaway volley is if you have just hit a very strong baseline ground stroke, causing your opponent to hit a very soft, shallow ball back to you. Recognize this situation and get to the ball quickly so that you are in position to hit a volley. Make sure that the ball is still above the height of the net. Find an angle that will make it virtually impossible for your opponent to hit it back.

The reaction volley is hit when you are at the net and a shot is coming straight at you. Take this shot as a backhand, making sure that your racket face stays perpendicular to the ground. It is more a block than a volley. Reaction volleys happen when your opponent hits a flat, hard shot right at you either because he or she is pressured for time and must swing fast to get a shot off or because he or she wanted to hit a fast shot. In either case, make sure that you are waiting with your racket in front of you in the ready position. When you see the ball coming right at you, simply block the shot and hold on to your racket.

PLAY CATCH

This is a partner drill. Players stand about 10 feet from the net on opposite sides of the court, facing each other (figure 5.7). No rackets are needed for this drill, just balls. One player is the feeder, the other is the catcher. The feeder uses an underhand toss to throw a ball to the catcher's forehand side. The catcher executes a split step on the feeder's release, steps across with the nondominant foot (for a right-hander, the left foot), and catches the ball with the dominant hand in front of the body and the back of the hand toward the back fence. The catcher's arm should be straight. Repeat 10 times and switch roles.

5.7 Play catch drill.

This drill can be done for the backhand as well. The feeder uses an underhand toss to throw a ball to the catcher's backhand side. The catcher executes a split step on the feeder's release, steps across with the dominant foot (for a right-hander, the right foot), and blocks the ball with the backside of the dominant hand in front of the body. Repeat 10 times and switch roles.

VOLLEY IN FRONT

This is a partner drill. Follow the same procedures as the catch drill, but the catcher should use a racket instead of the hand.

VOLLEY–VOLLEY

This is a partner drill. Players stand just inside the service line on opposite sides of the court (figure 5.8). The goal is to hit as many consecutive volleys to each other as possible. The split step is very important in this drill! Try not to let the ball bounce. You can start by just bumping the ball back and forth to each other. As you get better at it, move back a couple of feet from the service line and flatten out your volleys. Try to get to 20 consecutive hits without letting the ball touch the ground.

5.8   **Volley–volley drill.**

BRUTAL VOLLEY

This is a more difficult version of the volley–volley drill. In this drill, half volleys, regular volleys, putaway volleys, and reaction volleys are used. Players stand on opposite sides of the court at about midcourt. Use only half the court. Start with a ball out of the hand. Both players try to move in toward the net with each shot. After a rally is done, go back to midcourt and start again.

VOLLEY–GROUND STROKES

This is a partner drill. In this drill, one player should start at the net and the other at the baseline on opposite sides of the court. The net player hits volleys and the baseline player hits ground strokes. When you get to 20 consecutive hits, switch roles.

PASSING SHOT GAME

This is a partner game. In this game, one player starts at the net and the other at the baseline. Either player can start the point with a ball out of the hand. Three friendly shots must be hit before the point is played out. Play to seven points (must win by two points), then switch roles.

Set Point

Volleys enable you to take advantage of situations in which weight transfer is more effective than body rotation or racket work. The split step is extremely important in getting in position to hit a good volley. As you step out of your split step, try to step forward into the volley. With practice, you will learn to have a forward attitude when hitting volleys and overcome the fear of being at the net. Over time, your volley should become a very effective and fun shot to hit.

The next shot, the lob, is similar to a ground stroke. It can be hit on both the forehand and backhand sides. The main difference between a lob and a ground stroke is that lobs have a high trajectory.

Lob

The lob is a ground stroke that is usually hit from the baseline and is hit high and deep. There are many good reasons for hitting a lob. The most common use of a lob is when your opponent is at the net and you want to hit the ball over him or her or you want to make him or her hit a difficult overhead. Another good time to hit a lob is when you are pulled off the court in the middle of a point and you want to give yourself more time to recover. Other good reasons to hit lobs are if your opponent has a poor overhead; if your opponent does not handle high bouncing ground strokes well; if you want to throw a change-of-pace shot in there, as a response to a lob from your opponent; or if your opponent is facing the sun.

An effective lob should either neutralize an attack or put you on the offense in the point. Once you hit an effective lob, you are ready to attack with either a ground stroke, a volley, or an overhead.

Forehand and Backhand Lobs

As with ground strokes, the lob starts with a good ready position and a well-timed split step. For the forehand lob (figure 6.1), use the eastern grip. Turn your shoulders and take the racket back, below the anticipated point of contact. Make sure your knees are bent. Step forward with your left leg (if you are right-handed) to transfer your weight forward. Your feet should be more than shoulder-width apart. This will help you maintain balance.

Forehand Lob

6.1a Backswing.

6.1b Make contact.

Accelerate the racket head forward, making sure that you maintain a slightly open racket face. This open racket face makes the difference between a ground stroke and a lob. The more open the racket face, the higher the trajectory of the ball. However, if the racket face is too open, the ball will not travel forward very far. Contact the ball out in front of your body, below waist level. Finish the shot by following through forward and high. Your shoulders should have rotated so that your body is facing the court by the end of the shot.

For the backhand lob (figure 6.2), use the continental grip. Your nondominant hand should be at the throat as you pull the racket back for the backswing. Make sure you keep the racket low so that you can swing from low to high.

Backhand Lob

| 6.2a | **Backswing.** | 6.2b | **Make contact.** |

Step forward with your right leg (if you are right-handed). Keep your knees bent and your feet greater than shoulder-width apart. As you accelerate your racket forward, let go of the racket with your nondominant hand. It should stay behind you so that you can maintain your balance. Transfer your weight forward.

Contact the ball in front of you and below waist level. As with the forehand lob, it is important to contact the ball with an open racket face. Finish the shot by following through forward and high. To maintain control, your right shoulder (if you are right-handed) should be facing the other side of the court.

Putting underspin or topspin on the lob can be useful in certain situations. For example, if your opponent is at the net, a topspin lob may be useful because the ball will bounce away from your opponent. An underspin lob is useful in a defensive situation because it is easier for you to hit than a topsin lob.

Underspin Lob

The underspin lob is usually hit in defensive situations. The stroke does not take a lot of time to hit. It often is hit higher and lands deeper in the court than a topspin lob. It is a good shot to hit in emergency situations in which you need to buy yourself time to recover to a reasonable position in the court.

For the forehand underspin lob (figure 6.3), start with either an eastern or a continental grip. The continental grip will allow for a slightly more open racket face. From the split step, take your racket back as in a flat forehand lob. Your feet may be farther apart than in a flat forehand lob in order to main-

6.3   **Forehand underspin lob.**

tain balance while hitting balls that are lower. Your racket face should be slightly more open than for the flat lob. Generate underspin by slightly brushing down on the backside of the ball. Follow through high in the direction of the shot.

For the backhand underspin lob (figure 6.4), use the continental grip, which will open up the racket face. From the split step, take your racket back slightly, to about shoulder level, with the racket face open. Step in with your right foot and generate underspin by slightly brushing underneath the ball and following through toward the opposite side of the court.

6.4   **Backhand underspin lob.**

Topspin Lob

The topspin lob is more of an offensive shot. It is most commonly used when your opponent is at the net and you have time to execute a topspin lob. The trajectory of the shot is a bit lower than that of the underspin lob. It lets you hit a shot that is high enough to be out of your opponent's reach but bounces off the court quickly.

For the forehand topspin lob (figure 6.5), start with either an eastern or semi-western grip. The semi-western grip will allow for more topspin. From the split step, turn your shoulders and take your racket back in a looping arc so that it goes back to about shoulder height, then drops down below the ball. Contact should be made in front of the body and slightly higher than for the flat forehand lob. At contact, brush up on the backside of the ball so that topspin is generated. Follow through in this upward movement.

For the backhand topspin lob (figure 6.6), use a continental grip. Take the racket back as in a topspin backhand ground stroke. To hit a topspin lob, brush up on the back of the ball.

For the two-handed backhand topspin lob (figure 6.7), use a continental grip for your dominant hand and an eastern grip for your nondominant hand. Take your racket

6.5 **Forehand topspin lob.**

6.6 **Backhand topspin lob.**

6.7 **Two-handed backhand topspin lob.**

back as for the two-handed topspin backhand. Again, brush up on the backside of the ball to create topspin and add height to the shot.

Lob Volley

The lob volley (figure 6.8) is a very handy shot to know when both players are at the net. It is somewhat of a surprise tactic and should not be used too often. As the name implies, it is a volley (the ball is hit before it bounces) that goes over your opponent's head. It is especially useful when your opponent's momentum is moving forward.

The lob volley is hit in the same way as a regular volley, except at the last moment, open the racket face. Swing upward and through, thereby lifting the ball over your opponent. Make sure the shot is high enough and has enough forward momentum so that your opponent cannot hit an overhead.

6.8 **Lob volley.**

Picking a Lob

As mentioned before, lobs are very useful in certain situations or in creating certain situations. The following explains the most likely reasons to use each kind of lob.

The flat lob may be used for a variety of reasons, both offensive and defensive. It may be used to gain time so that you can recover to the middle of the court while the ball is in the air. It may be used when your opponent is at the net. It may be used simply to change the pace or rhythm of the point. It may be used because your opponent does not like to hit slow, high bouncing shots. The flat lob is a useful, versatile shot to have in your repertoire. It can serve a lot of purposes and is a relatively low-risk shot to hit.

The underspin lob is used mostly in defensive situations when you don't have a lot of time to hit a shot or you cannot get good balance from your position. For example, if your opponent is running you from side to side and you are barely reaching the ball, throw an underspin lob in there to give yourself time to recover. The underspin lob is a much easier shot to hit than the topspin lob and can get you out of a lot of bad situations!

The topspin lob is mostly used as an offensive shot, although sometimes it is used simply to change the pace of a rally. A common use of a topspin lob is when your opponent is at the net and you have enough time to hit a topspin lob over his or her head. Because of the topspin, you can give the ball a looping trajectory. This means that the ball should be just out of your opponent's reach as it bounces away from him or her. As previously mentioned, another reason to hit topspin lobs is to change the pace of a rally. The topspin gives the shot an extra kick after the bounce. It is a good tactic to use against players who do not like to hit high balls. It also pushes your opponent back behind the baseline, making it hard for him or her to attack.

The lob volley is used when both players are at the net. This situation is more common in doubles than in singles. The ball should go directly over the net person's head or slightly to the backhand side, sending him or her running toward the baseline. This usually creates a good situation for the player or team that hit the lob volley.

FEED DRILL

This is a partner drill. The feeder stands just inside the service line on one side. The hitter stands at the baseline on the other side. The feeder starts by feeding a ball to the hitter's forehand side. The hitter hits a flat forehand lob. The lob should go past the service line on the other side. Repeat 10 times, then switch roles. Repeat to the backhand side, then repeat for underspin and topspin lobs.

LOB-LOB

This is a partner drill. In this drill, players start at the baselines on opposite sides of the court. Hit different types of lobs to each other, each time trying to get it past the service line on the other side.

LOB EVERYTHING

This is a partner drill. Players start at the baselines on opposite sides of the court. One of the players can hit any type of shot (any pace, spin, and/or height). The other player must always hit lobs. Do this for 10 minutes, then switch roles.

6.9 Monkey in the middle.

MONKEY IN THE MIDDLE

Three people are needed for this drill. One player stands at each baseline and the third stands in the service box on either side (figure 6.9). This person is the "monkey." The player on the other side of the court from the monkey needs to hit lobs that are high and deep enough that the monkey cannot touch them. The monkey cannot go outside of the service box. The baseline player on the monkey's side cannot hit anything but lobs in order to avoid hurting the monkey. Rotate positions after the monkey touches the ball three times so that all three players can play each position.

LOB VOLLEY GAME

This is a partner game. Players start just inside the service lines on opposite sides of the court and start volleying to each other. After three volleys, either player is allowed to hit a lob volley at any time. Play the point out. This game should show you what can happen when the lob volley is hit in this situation. Play to seven points (win by two).

Set Point

The lob is an extremely useful shot to have in your tennis game. As you improve, you will find that lobs can help you create and get out of certain situations. Use offensive lobs, such as the topspin lob and the lob volley, to create situations for yourself or to get your opponent out of position. Use defensive lobs, such as the underspin lob, to get out of emergency situations, such as when your opponent is running you from side to side or if you are off balance.

As you practice the drills and games and your technique improves, you will find that using these shots and applying these tactics in your tennis game can make it a lot of fun! One of the shots used to counter the lob is the overhead smash, which is discussed in the next chapter.

Overhead Smash

The overhead smash is one of the most fun and spectacular shots to hit in tennis. It is usually hit at the net or midcourt off a lob. The stroke for this offensive shot is similar to that of a serve, with a couple of exceptions. In a more basic sense, the overhead smash is similar to an overhand throwing motion. With the proper technique, the overhead smash can be a very effective weapon in your game.

The overhead smash is an offensive shot hit off a lob. Instead of letting the lob bounce and hitting a ground stroke or another lob off it, it is much more beneficial to take it in the air and hit an overhead off it.

Executing the Overhead

Start in ready position 8 to 10 feet from the net. Hold the racket in a continental grip if you are comfortable with it. If not, use a grip between the eastern forehand grip and the continental grip, with the goal of slowly migrating to the continental grip.

Execute a split step, then turn your shoulders with both arms up (figure 7.1a). Bend the elbow on the arm holding the racket. Drop your right foot back (if you are right-handed) so that you are sideways to the net. Shift your weight to the right foot. Lean your upper body back as you turn your shoulders a bit more.

Drop the racket behind your back (figure 7.1b). Your left arm should be straight and high. This helps maintain balance and turn your shoulders. Your left hand can be used to track the ball. Make sure that you are always slightly behind the ball. Use a shuffle step if you need to move forward or backward to get behind the ball. Bend your knees so that your body is prepared to accelerate up.

7.1a   **Split step.**

7.1b   **Turn your shoulders and drop the racket.**

As you accelerate the racket forward and high to strike the ball, turn your upper body in the direction of the shot. Try to keep the elbow of the hitting arm high. Contact the ball slightly in front of your body and at the highest point you can reach (figure 7.1c). Your body and arm should be fully extended, and your body weight should be on the left foot. Keep your chin up at contact. If you put your head down, your whole body will go slightly down. After making contact, follow through by bringing the racket to the left side of your body (figure 7.1d). Your body weight should end up on the front foot.

One of the most important things to remember when hitting an overhead smash is to swing early enough that contact is made at the highest point possible. If you wait too long and try to hit the ball when it is too low, your hitting arm will not be fully extended at contact. This is probably the most common error made by players learning to hit the overhead.

7.1c **Make contact in front of your body and as high as you can reach.**

7.1d **Follow through to the other side of your body.**

A couple of aspects of the overhead smash differentiate it from the serve. (See chapter 9 for more about the serve.) First, the overhead smash is not hit off a toss—it is hit off a high shot. Therefore, you must make adjustments with the feet in order to get into the correct position to hit an effective overhead. Second, the start of the backswing is different. The serve requires a pendulum-like swing—the racket goes down, then up. For an overhead, however, the racket is immediately brought up next to the right side of the upper body. You may not have enough time to execute a pendulum-like swing when hitting an overhead, especially against a lob with a low trajectory.

Another important aspect of the overhead smash is the player's position while hitting it. If at all possible, keep both feet on the ground when hitting an overhead smash. This position helps maintain balance and keeps technique clean.

Scissors Jump Overhead Smash

Sometimes players jump in the air to hit overheads. This technique, called the scissors jump overhead smash, is required when the ball is slightly behind the player but an overhead is needed. This move is more of a thrust than a jump.

The scissors jump overhead smash (figure 7.2) is hit around midcourt off a good, deep lob. It is not as complicated as it sounds; it is a fairly natural motion in this situation.

Start in ready position 8 to 10 feet behind the net, holding the racket with a continental or eastern grip. After executing a split step, turn your shoulders. Both arms should be raised high. Bend the elbow of your racket arm. Drop your right foot back (if you are right-handed) farther than you would for a regular overhead smash. Your body weight should be on your right foot.

As you drop your racket behind your back, thrust off your right leg. When you perform this motion, your left leg will come off the ground as well. Your legs will naturally execute the scissors movement in the air in order to maintain balance. Your right leg will end up in front, while the left leg will end up behind you.

Accelerate the racket forward, toward the ball. Make contact slightly in front of or above your head. Make sure that your body and racket arm are at full extension at the point of contact. Turn your body toward the shot. Your upper body will lean back slightly due to the thrust upward while going backward.

After making contact, follow through to your left side and land on your left foot. To maintain balance, your right leg will be high and pointing forward. Your upper body will lean forward slightly as you recover from the follow-through.

Scissors Jump
Overhead Smash

| 7.2a | Shuffle step back to get in position. | 7.2b | Thrust off your back leg and accelerate the racket up toward the ball. |

As with the regular overhead smash, do not use a pendulum-like backswing. You have even less time to prepare to hit the scissors jump overhead smash!

Backhand Overhead Smash

The backhand overhead smash (figure 7.3) is one of the most athletic shots in tennis. Whenever possible, you should try to hit the over-head smash on the forehand side, but in some situations it might not be possible to run around the lob. In these situations, hit the backhand overhead smash.

Stand 8 to 10 feet from the net. Start in the ready position, hold-ing the racket with the continental grip. After you execute the split step and realize that you are not going to be able to hit an overhead smash on the forehand side, turn your shoulders as if showing the back of your shirt to your opponent. Use a fairly big step to drop your left foot back (if you are right-handed) so that your whole body is not turned. The shoulders should be turned more than the legs so that the legs are more or less sideways to the opponent, with the right leg behind the left leg.

Backhand Overhead Smash

7.3a	Turn your shoulders and prepare the racket.

7.3b	Make contact in front.

The hitting elbow should be so high that the racket points down. Keep your left hand on the throat of the racket as you take it back. Your upper body should be leaning back slightly as your hitting shoulder rises. All of your weight should be on the left foot.

As you accelerate the racket forward, thrust off the left leg. At contact, your body and hitting arm should be at full extension. Contact the ball slightly in front of your body. At this point, almost your entire back should be toward the net in order to maximize the efficiency of your arm.

Continue to swing the racket through the contact point toward your shot. Land on your left foot. Use your left arm and right leg to maintain balance. You can land on your right foot if your whole back was turned toward the net at contact.

Overhead Smash After a Bounce

This type of overhead smash is hit in the same way as a regular overhead smash except that you let the ball bounce before hitting it (figure 7.4). It is usually hit off a very high lob. The key to this overhead smash is getting prepared early and using quick footwork so that you can be right behind the ball, just waiting to eat it up!

First, let the ball bounce and prepare your racket as you would for a regular overhead. Make sure there is plenty of space so that as the ball reaches the appropriate height there is enough room for you to take a full swing. When the ball is as high as your racket can reach, execute an overhead smash.

Overhead Smash After a Bounce

7.4a   Let the ball bounce and prepare your racket.

7.4b   Hit the overhead smash.

Selecting an Overhead Smash

Different situations call for different types of overheads. It is important for you to recognize each situation so that you can choose the appropriate overhead. Your choice of overhead may depend on the type of lob your opponent hits, your position on the court, your opponent's position on the court, or even the weather conditions, such as wind or sun.

When executing a regular overhead smash, it is important to consider where you are on the court and what type of lob your opponent hit. Should you play offensively or defensively? If you are close to the net and your opponent hits a shallow lob, you should hit a more aggressive overhead smash, one with good pace and angle. If you find yourself at midcourt or deeper, you might want to hit an overhead smash that goes back to your opponent fairly deep and not so fast. This will give you time to recover and get closer to the net, maybe looking for an attack on the next shot.

Use the scissors jump overhead smash when the trajectory of the lob your opponent hit prevents you from making contact without leaving the ground. Because it takes a bit longer to recover from a jump smash than a regular smash, put a bit of spin on the shot to give yourself more time.

Execute the backhand overhead smash when your opponent hits the lob to your backhand side and you do not have enough time to run around it. Go ahead and hit the overhead in this situation; letting the ball bounce may create a more difficult situation. If you hit the backhand overhead shot, you make it more difficult for your opponent to recover to a good position.

Sometimes it is best to let the lob bounce before hitting the overhead smash. This shot can be used in several situations. Use it when your opponent hits an extremely high lob. Because it is so high, it will be difficult for you to judge its position and it will fall fast. In this case, it is less risky for you to let it bounce even though this will give your opponent time to set up. Another situation in which to let the lob bounce is when conditions are windy. Wind makes it difficult to judge lobs. You might also want to let the lob bounce if you are facing the sun.

CATCH THE FLY BALL

This is a partner drill. One player is the feeder, the other is the catcher. The feeder stands at the baseline. The catcher starts about 10 feet from the net. When the catcher runs up to the net and taps the net with his or her racket, the feeder hits a lob. The catcher uses shuffle steps to get into the correct overhead position and catches the ball with his or her non-dominant hand (figure 7.5). Repeat 10 times, then switch roles.

7.5   Catch the fly ball drill.

7.6   Hit the fly ball drill.

HIT THE FLY BALL

This partner drill is similar to the Catch the Fly Ball drill. One player is the feeder, the other is the catcher. The feeder stands at the baseline. The catcher starts about 10 feet from the net. When the catcher runs up to the net and taps the net with his or her racket, the feeder hits a lob. The catcher uses shuffle steps to get into the correct overhead position and hits an overhead smash off the lob (figure 7.6). Repeat 10 times, then switch roles.

THE T DRILL

This partner drill expands on the lessons learned in the Hit the Fly Ball drill. It starts the same way: the hitter runs to the net and taps it. The feeder hits a lob. The hitter executes an overhead smash. After the overhead smash is hit, the feeder hits two more balls, one to the hitter's forehand side and the next to the hitter's backhand side (figure 7.7). The hitter hits volleys off the feeds. Repeat 4 times for a total of 12 shots, then switch roles. Make sure you split step on the volleys.

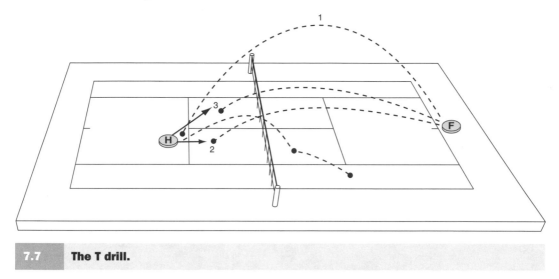

7.7　**The T drill.**

LOB AND OVERHEAD CONTROL

In this partner drill, control is practiced on both the lob and the overhead. Players start on opposite sides of the court (figure 7.8). The player hitting lobs (the lobber) starts at the baseline; the player hitting overhead smashes (the smasher) starts at the net. The lobber hits a lob to the smasher. The smasher gets into correct position and hits an overhead smash. The lobber tries to return each overhead smash with another lob.

Both players try to keep the ball in play, not hitting anything too hard or too fast. The smasher should work on getting in the correct position and being prepared early so that the swing can be controlled. The lobber should work on correctly executing split steps to get into the right position to hit the next lob. Hit eight consecutive shots, then switch roles.

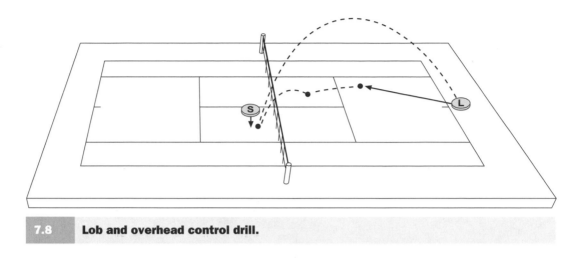

7.8   **Lob and overhead control drill.**

TWO-ON-THREE

In this fast-paced game, ground strokes, volleys, lobs, and overhead smashes are used by all the players. Three players spread out along the baseline; the other two players stand at the net on the other side of the court (figure 7.9). The point starts when one of the baseline players drop-hits a lob. One of the net players returns the lob by hitting an overhead. After this overhead shot, players can use any type of shot. Players do not have to stay in their original positions. If the side with two players loses the point, one of those players is replaced by one of the baseline players. If the side with three players loses the point, all three must do either 10 push-ups or 10 crunches. The object of the game is to stay on the net side (the side with two players) and get fit. Play for 10 minutes and take a rest.

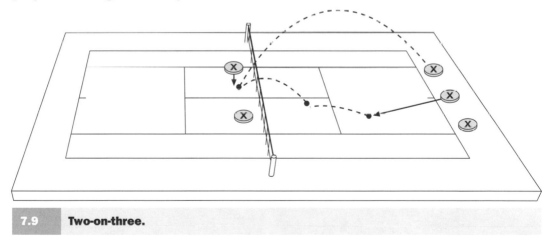

7.9   **Two-on-three.**

Set Point

The overhead smash is all about confidence. If you know you will hit it well going into the shot, you most likely will. If you doubt yourself before each overhead, you probably will not do as well. Practice is the only thing that will give you the confidence you need to do well.

From the mighty and powerful overhead smash, we go to the sneaky and soft drop shot in the next chapter.

Drop Shot

The drop shot is a big weapon when executed correctly and at the right time. When your opponent is least expecting it or when he or she would have to run a good distance to reach it, that is the time to use the drop shot.

A drop shot is softly hit with underspin while the player is as close to the net as possible. Its main purpose is to catch your opponent off guard, especially when he or she is not ready to move forward into the court. Another purpose for the drop shot is to draw your opponent up to the net.

The whole effect of a drop shot on the ball is that it slows down the ball considerably. As the executor of the drop shot, your job is to absorb a lot of the momentum and send it back with underspin. Therefore, the faster the oncoming shot is, the more difficult it will be to hit a drop shot off it.

A good analogy to the drop shot is the free throw in basketball. A basketball player uses touch and arc when shooting a free throw. The same things are important when hitting a drop shot. In fact, when hitting a drop shot, it may help to imagine a basketball hoop on the other side of the net.

Forehand and Backhand Drop Shots

We begin with the forehand drop shot (figure 8.1). Stand around the service line when practicing drop shots and start in the ready position. Hold the racket in an eastern forehand or continental grip. Turn your shoulders as if to hit a forehand ground stroke, but make the backswing short and high. Step in with the left foot (if you are right-handed) and make sure your feet are more than shoulder-width apart to maintain good balance. Bend your knees. Your whole body should be poised to absorb contact!

Before contact, the racket arm should be slightly bent and the racket face should be slightly open. Make contact slightly in front of and to the side of your body. At contact, hit the ball slightly downward and forward, almost as if to stop the ball. Follow through slightly upward, as if to dish the ball back over the net. This helps put underspin on the ball.

Forehand Drop Shot

8.1a Absorb the contact.

8.1b Follow through.

For the backhand drop shot (figure 8.2), hold the racket in a continental grip. On the backswing, use your left hand (if you are right-handed) to hold the throat of the racket for control. Again, the backswing should be short and high. A short backswing prevents the racket from building too much momentum. Your knees should be bent.

Step forward with the right foot (if you are right-handed) and release the racket with your left hand as you swing forward. Your whole body should be ready to absorb the impact of the ball. The racket arm should be straight. Make contact slightly in front of and to the side of your body. The racket head should be open so that you can put underspin on the ball. Follow through toward the shot, keeping an open racket face.

The most important thing to remember on both your forehand and backhand drop shots is to follow through, but try not to follow through too fast or else your racket head speed will be too fast. This will result in sending the ball back faster than you intended.

Backhand Drop Shot

| 8.2a | Make contact. | 8.2b | Follow through. |

When directing the drop shot, you have two choices: crosscourt or down the line. The crosscourt drop shot is a much longer shot to hit than a down-the-line drop shot. Another important thing to keep in mind is the height of the net. When hitting crosscourt shots, you will go over the lowest part of the net. When hitting a down-the-line drop shot, you will be going over the highest part of the net.

Drop Volley

The drop volley (figure 8.3) is a volley that is hit as a drop shot. Usually a drop volley is hit off a relatively low incoming shot; high shots should be hit with a putaway volley. The idea for the drop volley is the same as for the regular drop shot. A drop volley may be a bit more difficult to hit because the ball has not bounced, therefore the ball may be traveling relatively fast.

8.3 **The drop volley.**

The technique for the drop volley is more or less the same as for the drop shot. The only difference is that you may have to get down lower (bend your knees more and spread your feet apart for good balance) and you may have to absorb more at impact (the racket may have more of a downward movement at impact).

The drop volley is a good shot to hit when you find yourself very close to the net with your opponent behind the baseline and you want to hit a ball that is below the level of the net. If the ball is higher than the net, always try to hit a putaway volley!

The Element of Surprise

The drop shot should be used mostly as a surprise element; do not try to use the drop shot every single opportunity you get. It is a risky shot to hit. Taking so much pace off the ball is not an easy thing to do and you might miss more than you make. Also, if you hit a drop shot too high or too deep, you are suddenly in an extremely defensive position.

Here are some good situations in which to use a drop shot:

■ Your opponent is deep in the court, almost near the back fence, and has just hit a shot to you that is not too deep and is easy to handle. This might be a good time to try a drop shot. Hit a drop shot that makes your opponent run the farthest distance (the diagonal shot).

■ You are playing a very tired opponent. Watching a drop shot fall is a psychologically devastating feeling for a tired player. Again, make sure you hit the drop shot diagonally away from your opponent.

■ You are playing an opponent who does not like to run forward or does not like to volley. Usually these two characteristics go hand in hand. You will have a big advantage if you can make players unwillingly go to the net.

■ Another situation in which drop shots are useful is before or after a lob. With this tactic, you can make your opponent run back and forth the length of his or her side of the court!

There are a couple of things to watch for when hitting drop shots or drop volleys. Watch for the counter drop shot. As you hit your drop shot, watch how your opponent reacts to it. Is your opponent going to get there in plenty of time? If so, be ready for anything. Is your opponent barely going to get to the ball? If so, watch for a very short response or a counter drop shot. A player who is reaching for a ball, especially a very short ball, may be able to hit only a short shot back.

Also, don't use the drop shot as a desperation shot. One of the most powerful parts of the drop shot is the element of surprise. If you use it every single time you have a chance, your opponent will catch on and start running before you even hit the shot!

DROP-HIT DROP SHOT

This drill can be done alone. Stand about 10 feet from the net. Drop hit drop shots from this position (figure 8.4). Your goal is to make the ball bounce four times before reaching the other service line. Be sure to follow through and put underspin on the ball. Hit 12, then switch to your backhand.

8.4 **Drop-hit drop shot drill.**

CATCH THE BALL ON THE RACKET

This is a partner drill that can be done in any open space. One player is the feeder, the other is the catcher. To start, players face each other, about 15 feet apart. The feeder underhand tosses the ball to the catcher, who tries to catch the ball on a racket with minimal bouncing (figure 8.5). The key is to keep the racket moving in the direction of the ball until you can stop the ball. This drill helps you get a feel for absorbing and stopping the momentum of the ball. Try it 10 times and then switch roles.

8.5 **Catch the ball on the racket drill.**

DROP SHOT PARTNER DRILL

One player is the feeder, the other is the hitter. The feeder stands about five feet from the net. The hitter starts at the baseline on the other side of the court. When the feeder drop hits a drop shot, the hitter sprints up to the ball and hits a drop shot off it before it bounces twice. The feeder should change the difficulty of the initial shot according to the hitter's speed. After hitting the drop shot, the hitter backpedals to the baseline. Repeat 10 times on the forehand, then switch roles. Repeat with the backhand side.

DROP SHOT TARGET DRILL

This drill is similar to the drop shot partner drill. The only difference is that in this drill, a target is put very close to the net. A wastebasket is always a good target for this drill, as it gives the image of a basketball hoop on the other side of the net. Both players hit drop shots. The feeder uses the drop shot to feed the ball to the hitter. The hitter hits a drop shot, aiming for the target on the feeder's side of the net. Repeat 10 times each for the forehand down the line, forehand crosscourt, backhand down the line, and backhand crosscourt.

CAT AND MOUSE

This partner drill is similar to the figure eights drill in chapter 4 (page 39) except that it uses drop shots. Players stand at the service lines on opposite sides of the court. One player is the "down-the-line" player; this player hits drop shots parallel to the singles sideline. The other player is the "crosscourt" player; this player hits drop shots from his or her deuce side to the other's ad side, and vice versa (figure 8.6). Try to hit each shot as close to the net on the other side as possible. This is a difficult drill as there is little recovery time between shots. Play for about five minutes, then switch roles. Try to get to a rally of 10. As you get better, you will find that your shots are very close to the net and that the crosscourt player needs to use very extreme angles.

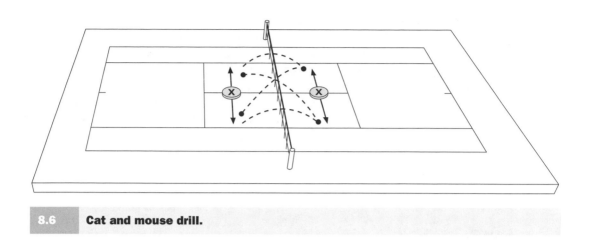

8.6   **Cat and mouse drill.**

PICK LINE GAME

This game is named after Kat Pick, one of my assistant coaches, who came up with the game. You need some white athletic tape for this game. Put four pieces of tape to extend the service line out to the doubles sidelines as shown in figure 8.7.

This game can be played with two or four people. Players start at their respective service lines (one-on-one or two-on-two). Start with a soft underhand feed and play the point out. The boundaries are the extended service line and the doubles sidelines. You will find that hitting angled, crosscourt drop shots and very short down-the-line drop shots will work to your advantage. The first player to get 11 points, with a margin of 2 points, wins.

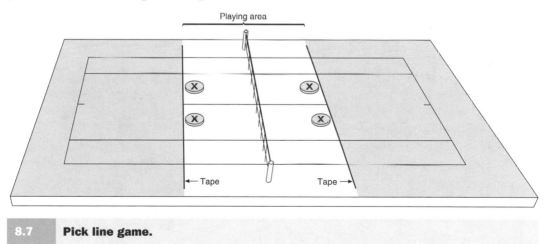

8.7   **Pick line game.**

Set Point

As you practice the drop shot, you will find that it is one of the most fun and beautiful shots to hit in tennis. It can help you set up situations, change the momentum of a match, and make your other shots more effective. The important thing to remember is not to overuse it in match play or it will lose the element of surprise.

We are finally ready to learn one of the most important and probably most difficult shots in this game: the serve. In the next chapter, the service motion, different types of serves, and serve placement are discussed.

Serve

The basic purpose of the serve is to start a point. When you first learn to serve, you should work on consistency, not speed or power. If you cannot get the serve in, it won't do you any good to hit it fast. It takes a lot of practice to be proficient at serving. It's a good idea to get a basket full of balls, go to the court, and practice your serve whenever you can.

The serve is hit from behind the baseline, either left or right of the center mark. For it to be a legal serve, you must hit the ball before it bounces, and the serve must land in the diagonal service box on the opposite side. For each point, the server has two chances to get the serve in. If the server cannot execute a legal serve in two tries, it is called a double fault and the point goes to the receiver.

Simplified Serve

The simplified serve is a good place to start if you have never served before. What makes it simplified is that it cuts out some of the starting motion. The advantage is that it is a much easier motion to coordinate. The disadvantage is that the racket head will not have as much momentum going into the contact point. However, it is a perfectly legal and legitimate serve and a good starting point for beginners.

Start with the stance. If you are right-handed, your left foot should be in front, just behind the baseline, pointed toward the right net post. Your left foot should be behind your right foot, parallel to the baseline. Your feet should be about shoulder-width apart (figure 9.1a).

Hold your racket in an eastern forehand grip, a continental grip, or somewhere in between. It is fine to use the eastern forehand grip as long as the goal is to move to the continental grip eventually. Put your racket over your shoulder and down your back with the elbow high. Your palm should be to your ear (figure 9.1b).

For the toss, use your thumb, index finger, and middle finger to hold the ball in your left hand. Hold the ball as though you were holding a live bird—you don't want to squeeze it too hard, but if you don't hold on to it, it will fly away. Your arm should be relaxed in front of your left leg. Your knees should be slightly bent because you will be using your whole body, not just your arm, to toss the ball. Gradually accelerate your tossing arm up and let go of the ball when

9.1a Serving stance.   **9.1b** Racket behind the back.

your arm reaches a bit above head height (figure 9.1c). Do not flick your wrist; this will cause you to lose control of the ball. Your arm should be extended. At no time during the upward phase of the toss should your tossing arm flex. Be sure to keep your tossing arm up. The ball should go slightly higher than where you can reach with your racket and slightly forward so that when you hit the ball, you can have your body weight behind it. At this point, your body weight should be on your back foot, and your knees should be bent so that your whole body is ready to thrust upward and forward.

Now for the swing, accelerate the racket up to meet the ball (figure 9.1d). When you make contact, your hitting arm should be fully extended and contact should be made slightly in front and to the right of your body.

9.1c   **Ball toss.**

9.1d   **Reach up and make contact.**

Keep your chin up at contact and through the follow through. The racket face should face the opposite side of the court at contact. Your body weight should transfer from the back foot to the front foot. The follow-through should go across the body and finish on your right side. At the finish, your arms should form an X in front of your body, your racket arm over your tossing arm.

You may land on either foot. If you land on your right foot, it should come down after you have made contact with the ball. Legally, you cannot step on the baseline or into the court until after you have made contact with the ball. You can, however, cross the plane before contact.

Full Motion Serve

The full motion serve (figure 9.2) is basically the same as the simplified serve except that there is a bit more movement before contact so that the racket will have more momentum at contact.

Position the feet the same as for the simplified serve. The arms, however, start differently. Both arms should be in front of you and relaxed. Swing your racket arm down and up as if it were a pendulum, then turn your shoulders and drop the racket down your back. Make sure your elbow is high.

As you move your hitting arm down and up in the pendulum motion, your tossing arm should start its upward movement. Just as in the simplified serve, the tossing arm remains straight throughout the toss. Release the ball a bit above head level and keep your arm up. Your toss should go slightly higher than the highest point you can reach with your racket.

Accelerate your racket upward and forward to contact the ball at the highest point you can reach. Your hitting arm should be fully extended and contact should be made slightly in front of your body. The follow-through and finish are the same as for the simplified serve.

Full Motion Serve

| 9.2a | Serving stance. | 9.2b | Ball toss. | 9.2c | Contact and follow-through. |

Slice Serve

The slice serve (figure 9.3), although more difficult to hit than the full motion serve, is a bit less complicated than the topspin serve. Basically, it is a serve that puts sidespin on the ball, and the swing can go wide. With practice, the added spin will give you more control of placement and accuracy.

To hit the slice serve, you must use a continental or eastern backhand grip. You can use either the simplified service motion or the full service motion. The ball toss should be a bit to the right and a bit closer to your body than for a regular serve. The major difference between the slice serve and the flat serve is where you contact the ball. Imagine the face of a clock on the ball. For the slice serve, hit the ball at 2 o'clock. Just after ball contact, snap your wrist a bit toward the left.

Slice Serve

| 9.3a | Ball toss. | 9.3b | Reach up and make contact. |

The slice serve (short and wide) is especially useful on the deuce side as a surprise serve. After serving most of your serves down the T, your opponent probably will not be ready for a slice serve out wide. The disadvantage of this serve, however, is apparent if you are playing against an opponent who likes to hit angles: A player who likes to hit angles will use your angle to hit a severely angled shot back to you.

Topspin Serve

The topspin serve (figure 9.4) is a bit more difficult to hit than the slice serve. Many advanced players use the topspin serve as their second serve because it is more dependable than a flat serve. Just like a topspin forehand, it will have a relatively higher trajectory, dip sharply during flight, then take a high bounce. This kind of heavy ball provides good net clearance and will prevent the ball from sailing out of bounds.

Topspin Serve

| 9.4a | Ball toss. | 9.4b | Reach up and make contact. |

Use a continental or eastern backhand grip for the topspin serve. Toss the ball a bit to the left and a bit closer to your body than for a regular serve. This will allow you to come over the ball with the racket. Imagine the face of the clock again. Ball contact occurs between 12 o'clock and 1 o'clock (figure 9.5). The wrist snap should be made straight down.

The topspin serve (also called the kick serve) is a good serve to use against an opponent who does not like to hit high balls. The topspin is a dependable second serve. A disadvantage to the topspin serve is that if it is hit short, a good player will be all over it.

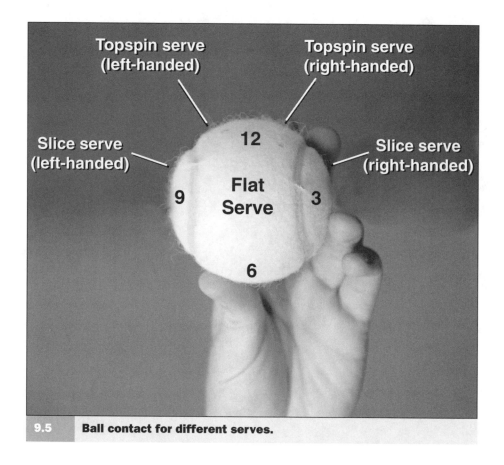

Topspin serve (left-handed)

Topspin serve (right-handed)

Slice serve (left-handed)

Slice serve (right-handed)

12

Flat Serve

9   3

6

9.5   Ball contact for different serves.

Placing the Serve

Because the serve is used to start the point, it gives the server a big advantage. The server gets to choose where and how to start the point. This advantage allows you to exploit your opponent's weaknesses. Here are some examples of where you can serve and why to serve there (see also figure 9.6).

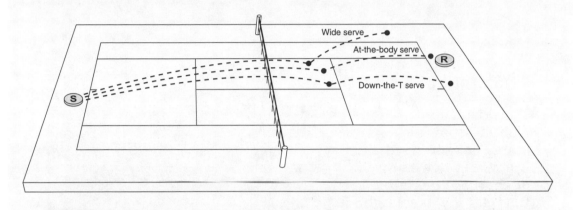

| **9.6** | **Serve placement.** |

■ The down-the-T serve goes straight down the center service line. It is a good serve to use, especially on the deuce (right) side, because it goes to your opponent's backhand, which usually is a weaker shot for your opponent. Another advantage is that it doesn't give your opponent a lot of time to react because it is the shortest distance from the server to the service box. Another advantage is that it goes over the lowest part of the net. (The net is 36 inches high at the center as opposed to 42 inches high at the ends.) It also is a good shot to use against someone who likes to produce angles and is skilled at doing so. Since this serve does not give your opponent any angles, it makes it more difficult for your opponent to generate any. A disadvantage is that because the distance is shorter, it is easier to hit it long, resulting in a service fault.

■ The wide serve, as the name implies, goes out wide. It can effectively be used on the ad (left) side because again, that's where your opponent's backhand is. Use the wide serve if your opponent is not so good at running out wide and cutting off angles or at hitting shots on the run. This serve opens up the court for you. Do not use this serve too much against opponents who like to hit angled shots.

91

■ The at-the-body serve is an underrated serve. This is an extremely valuable serve to have in your arsenal, as not many opponents will be able to be aggressive off a jamming serve. This is a good serve to hit against players who love to run after balls. This takes away their strength. Another good reason to hit this serve is if you are playing against someone with long limbs who finds it difficult to get out of the way.

TOSS DRILL

This drill can be done alone. Assume the correct stance for the serve. Put the racket down in front of the baseline, a bit to the right if you are right-handed or a bit to the left if you are left-handed. Place the racket so the head points toward the net and the grip points toward the back fence. With your nondominant hand, toss the ball and let it land. The goal is to have the toss land on the strings of the racket (figure 9.7).

9.7 **Toss drill.**

TRAP THE BALL

This drill can be done alone. Assume the correct stance for a serve, facing a wall or fence. With the racket behind your dominant shoulder and your elbow bent as if throwing a ball, toss the ball with your nondominant hand, reach up with your racket and gently trap the ball between the racket strings and the wall or fence (figure 9.8). Your hitting arm should be in full extension.

SHORT SERVES

This drill can be done alone. Instead of serving from the baseline, serve from the service line. This helps you concentrate on your technique instead of thinking about hitting the ball hard. Serve at least 20 on each side before moving back to the baseline.

9.8 Trap the ball drill.

TARGET SERVES

This drill can be done alone. Set up cones or ball pyramids (one tennis ball on top of a base of three tennis balls) in three positions in the service box: down the middle of the T, in the middle of the box, and out wide (figure 9.9). Before attempting each serve, make sure you pick one target and go for it. If you hit the target, fix it before the next attempt. Perform five attempts at each target before moving on to the next target.

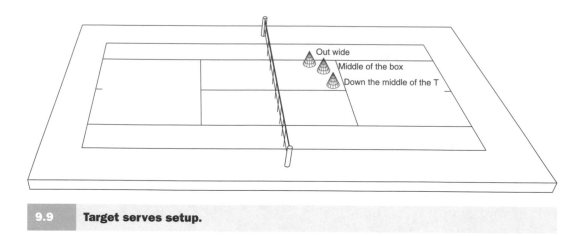

| 9.9 | **Target serves setup.** |

SPIN IT!

This drill can be done alone. This is a good drill for practicing second serves. Try to hit the serve as high as you can, using a regular service motion and a lot of topspin. This will help you practice the topspin, or kick, serve.

Set Point

The serve is one of the most complicated strokes in tennis. It takes a lot of practice, practice, practice to get a dependable serve. It is also one of the most important strokes in the game. It is important to achieve consistency on the serve before trying to hit it with increased power. Use the natural progression of working from the simplified serve to the full motion serve to spin serves to learn the correct technique. And, most important of all, be patient with yourself!

After the serve comes the return of serve. In the next chapter, you will learn to return serve and to understand the different types of returns.

10

CHAPTER

Return of Serve

The return of serve is a regular ground stroke, but it can be difficult to execute against an effective server. An effective server will get a high percentage of first serves in and will keep you guessing as to what type of serve is coming. The keys to returning consistently are waiting in the correct place, keeping your feet moving, and taking a short backswing.

There are different ways you can return serve, according to the serve or the type of player you are up against.

The return of serve is a very important part of the game because it is a shot that can determine whether you are offensive or defensive in the point. A deep return is most important in establishing yourself within a point. When you win a game as the returner, it is called a "break" in service.

Bisect the Angle

Three skills become increasingly important when returning service: waiting in the correct position on the court, having quick feet, and keeping your backswing short.

The return of serve requires a very important, basic understanding of how to position yourself in the optimal place on the court. This "rule" is called bisecting the angle. When you are at the baseline, you should position yourself in the middle of all possible shots that can be hit to you.

What does this mean? Let's say that you have just hit a ball to your right-handed opponent's deep backhand. Now you want to find the optimal place for you to position yourself so that you are in the middle of all possible return shots. On your right, the farthest you will need to run in is up to the deuce-side singles sideline. On your left, the farthest you will need to run is several feet past the ad-side singles sideline. This is dictated by the angles that are available to your opponent. Therefore, the middle is a couple of feet to the left of the centermark (figure 10.1). That is where you should wait for the next shot.

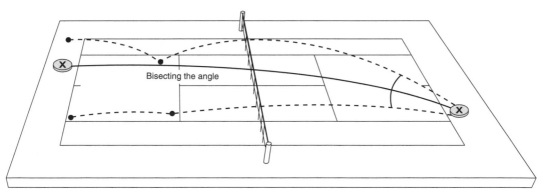

10.1 Bisecting the angle.

How does this apply to the return of serve? The return of serve is like any other ground stroke. Think about where the shot is coming from. If you are returning on the deuce side, the serve is coming from your opponent's deuce side. That means that the court is open or angled on your deuce side. The farthest you might have to laterally run to the left is up to the center service line. The farthest you might have to laterally run to the right is a few feet past the doubles sideline. This means that the middle for returning serves on the deuce side is approximately a bit to the left of the singles sideline (figure 10.2). The same rationale applies to the ad side. How hard your opponent serves the ball will dictate how close to the service line you should be. On the average, you want to be around the baseline.

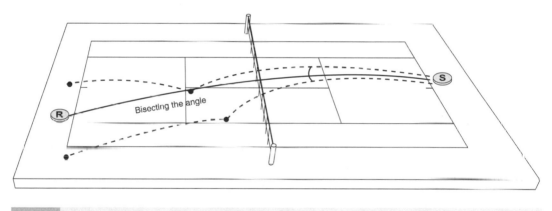

Bisecting the angle

10.2 **Bisecting the angle on service return.**

Basic Return

It is very important to keep your feet moving when returning serve (figure 10.3a), especially against a player who places serves well. This helps time the split step and, subsequently, movement to the ball. When returning serve, think of yourself as a boxer who hops around. Your body weight should be forward as you make contact with the ball.

A short backswing (figure 10.3b) is especially useful against a hard server. When the serve is coming at you fast, there is no time to take your racket back all the way as in a regular ground stroke. You must abbreviate your backswing, then transfer your weight forward and follow through. If your backswing is too big, you may get caught with your weight back and your contact point will be behind your body.

Basic Return

| 10.3a | Use quick feet. |

| 10.3b | Use a short backswing. |

The Chip and Charge

The chip and charge (figure 10.4) is a very aggressive return. It is an attack that usually is followed immediately by a movement to the net to finish the point with a volley or overhead shot.

The slice forehand or backhand is used to start the chip and charge. This is the chip part. Abbreviate the backswing. Hit the ball way in front of you so that you can lean into it. The follow-through should take you forward to the net. Follow through in the direction of the shot and charge the net!

The chip and charge is a useful tool to use. It does, however, take a tremendous amount of practice to be proficient at it. The purpose of the chip and charge is to put a lot of pressure on the server, as the returner displays an offensive, attacking attitude. The chip and charge should be used by players whose strengths are the volley and the overhead. It should especially be used against players who have a weak passing shot or lob.

Chip and Charge

10.4a The chip.

10.4b The charge.

Returning Against a Hard Server

Against a hard server, two things can be done to make your job as the returner a bit easier. First, stand farther back. This will buy you some time to react. Second, shorten your backswing. A shorter backswing makes clean contact with the ball much easier. It is almost as though you are going to hit a volley.

Returning Against a Soft Server

Many players have a hard time returning short or soft serves because they try to do way too much with it every single time. Players will unknowingly take a much bigger risk on a soft serve than if they were returning a regularly paced serve. Don't burden yourself with the pressure of feeling like you have to win the point right off the return. Instead, go for a higher-percentage shot, crosscourt and deep.

Returning Against a Serve and Volleyer

Against a player who likes to serve and volley, you can do several things. First, try hitting a passing shot outright. A passing shot is one that is untouched and goes right by the net player. This is often not an easy task to accomplish, especially off a good serve. Second, try to set yourself up for an easier passing shot by hitting a low return at the incoming server's feet. This can often be accomplished by hitting a ball with topspin, which will give you the desired trajectory. This will cause the server to have to volley up to you, and you can go for a passing shot off this shot. Third, try to hit a lob off the return. This is a good option against servers who don't have a good overhead or who don't have a good split step after the serve.

Returning Against a Baseliner

Against a solid baseline player, play high-percentage tennis by hitting the return deep and crosscourt. There are three reasons why hitting crosscourt is much safer than hitting down the line off a return: the net is the lowest in the middle (36 inches in the middle, 42 inches at the net posts); the court is longer diagonally so that you can reduce errors of length; and you will make a lot more errors changing the direction of the ball. Since the serve is coming from crosscourt, you don't have to change the direction of the ball when returning crosscourt.

MINI-SERVES AND RETURNS

This is a partner drill. One player is the server, the other is the returner. The server serves a moderately paced serve from the service line. The returner executes a split step, takes a very short backswing, and hits the return right off the bounce, almost as if blocking it, then follows through. Do 20 on each side, then switch roles.

SERVE–RETURN GAME

This game requires a server and a returner. Place a line of balls parallel to and about two feet inside the baseline. Each point consists of a serve and a return. Table 10.1 shows the scoring system. Although the scoring system seems to favor the returner, it isn't easy to return serve. Play to 11 points, then switch roles. Next play the game on the ad side.

Table 10.1

SCORING FOR THE SERVE–RETURN GAME

Outcome of point	Points awarded
Server misses serve	1 point for returner
Server makes serve, returner cannot hit a legal return	1 point for server
Server makes serve, returner hits legal return that bounces between the line of balls and baseline	3 points for returner
Server makes serve, returner hits legal return anywhere else in the singles court	1 point for returner

QUEEN OR KING OF THE COURT

Three or more players can play this game. One player starts as the queen or king. The others are the challengers; they are trying to overthrow the queen or king. The first challenger starts on the deuce side and serves to the queen or king. Just as in a regular point, the challenger gets two chances to hit a legal serve. If the challenger wins the point, he or she starts another point from the ad side. If the challenger loses the point, it is the next challenger's turn. The next challenger starts from the deuce side. If a challenger wins both a deuce point and an ad point in the same turn, he or she takes over as the queen or king. The overthrown king or queen joins the challenger line.

Set Point

The return of serve is one of the most important shots in tennis. It is important to remember a few key concepts when returning serve. First, make sure you are positioned correctly in the court. Second, make sure your feet are moving so that you can execute a well-timed split step. Third, turn your shoulders and take your racket back quickly and efficiently. Practice these three things every time you return serve and you should be able to cut down on errors as well as produce solid returns that give you the upper hand at the start of the point.

Now that you know all the basic tennis skills (grips, footwork, ground strokes, volleys, lobs, overheads, drop shots, serves, and returns of serve), you are ready to move on to the strategy of singles and doubles play. In the next chapter we will start with singles tactics.

Singles Tactics

As you improve your technique, tactics become more important in your tennis development. There are some basic strategies that anyone should follow in order to be successful. As these primary concepts become second nature to you, you can fine-tune your tactics based on your particular strengths and weaknesses, as well as your opponent's strengths and weaknesses. In this chapter, I discuss some basic strategies that should be the foundation of your tennis game and more specific strategies, such as the serve and volley.

As you put your tactics together and get better at putting them to use at the right times, you will see that tennis can be quite fun at a whole other level. It's fun to feel that a certain tactic is effective against a particular player or that your strengths fit well with a specific tactic.

Basic Strategies

There are some basic strategies that a tennis player at any level should follow. I refer to them as basic because they can be and should be integrated into any style of play. They should be used in every match, no matter what your playing style—baseliner, serve and volleyer, all court, or moonballer.

Playing the Percentages

Tennis is a percentage game. The player who takes fewer risks (and therefore selects shots that are more likely to go in) will most likely win the point. This is especially true at the beginner and intermediate levels. It may sound simple, but it is not always easy to do. It is very tempting to try to hit the winning shot. Follow these concepts to play high-percentage tennis.

First, go for consistency rather than power and speed. This cannot be overstated. I see too many players go for a fast-swinging shot and commit an unforced error because increasing the speed of the racket head alters their technique. At most levels of tennis, the player who makes fewer mistakes (not the player who hits more winners) will win the match.

Second, go crosscourt, especially off a crosscourt shot (figure 11.1). There are three big reasons to go crosscourt off a crosscourt shot:

1. The net is 6 inches lower in the middle (36 inches) than at the posts (42 inches).
2. The diagonal distance is longer than the down-the-line (straight) distance, which gives you more court to hit into.
3. It is much, much more difficult to change the direction of an incoming shot than to hit it back where it came from.

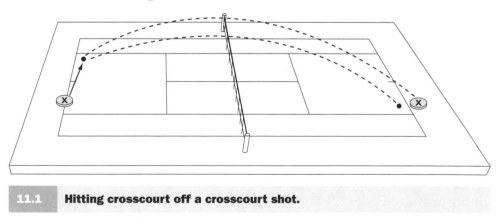

11.1 **Hitting crosscourt off a crosscourt shot.**

Third, aim high. You should not try to hit shots that skim right over the net. Aim at least five feet over the net when hitting a ground stroke. Not only will you cut the risk of hitting the ball into the net, you will be able to push your opponent farther back into the court, making it difficult for your opponent to attack your shots.

Bisecting the Angle

As mentioned in chapter 10, the concept of bisecting the angle is very important to understand when in position at the baseline. By figuring out where the middle is for each incoming shot, you put yourself in position to be able to get to a higher-percentage shot. Of course, this does not mean that from now on you will be able to get to every single shot; it just means that you are in the middle of all the possibilities for that particular situation.

Approaching the Net

Getting into position at the net is a bit different than getting into position at the baseline. At the net, time becomes more crucial because you do not have nearly as much of it to react to the shot. At the net, position yourself so that you can cover the shot that has the shortest distance to travel. That is, cover your opponent's down-the-line shot. For example, if your opponent is about to hit from his or her deuce side, scoot over to your left a bit so that you can cover the down-the-line shot.

It also is very important to close in at the net for a couple of reasons. First, if you are too far from the net, you will have to hit most of your volleys up and over the net instead of above the net. Being in position to hit volleys above the net is a much more offensive position than hitting them below the net. Second, it cuts down on the time your opponent has to react to your shot.

Of course, your opponent may try to hit a lob over your head. If this does happen, hit an overhead if you can or run down the shot. But don't stand in the middle of the court (called no man's land) in order to avoid the lob. This puts you in a vulnerable position, as you will be hitting a lot of shots off your shoelaces. Hitting balls off of your shoelaces is difficult, especially in the middle of the court, because the net is relatively high to you.

The approach shot (figure 11.2) is a transition shot that lets you come from the baseline to the net. The approach shot is usually hit off a weak or short shot from your opponent. For an effective approach shot, hit it early so that the contact point is not too low. The most important aspect of the approach shot is to hit it deep and down the line. Hitting a deep approach shot not only makes it difficult for your opponent to hit a passing shot, it gives you time to close in at the net. Going down the line is important so that you can follow straight in and get into position at the net. If you hit an approach shot cross court, you not only have to close in at the net diagonally (which is a longer distance than running straight in), but it also gives your opponent passing shot angles.

Approach Shot

| 11.2a | Hit the approach shot from the baseline. |

| 11.2b | Approach the net and hit a volley. |

Playing Types

As we incorporate the basic strategies discussed, the next step is understand what types of strategies you can use. This section describes some common playing types (see table 11.1).

The baseliner stays at the baseline and hits ground strokes. This is a common strategy that is used at all levels of tennis. The baseliner usually has reliable and sometimes aggressive ground strokes, is fit, and usually does not come to the net unless he or she has to. The baseliner is able to create situations from the baseline using accuracy and angles. The baseliner is usually good at hitting passing shots and returning serves.

The serve and volleyer, as you may have guessed, serves and immediately comes into the net to volley. This type of player usually

Table 11.1

Type of player	Strengths	Weaknesses	Counter strategies
Baseliner	Ground strokes, patience	Doesn't like net volleys	Drop shots; make the baseliner come to the net
Serve and volleyer	Serve, volley, overheads; very athletic	Consistency off ground strokes	Hit returns at the serve and volleyer's shoelaces; good lobs; moonballing
All court	Proficient in all strokes	No glaring weaknesses	Moonballing; take away the offense
Moonballer	Ground strokes, lobs; very patient and fit	Doesn't like the net; volleys and overheads	Drop shots; controlled aggression

has a strong first serve and a pressing second serve, as well as a great volley and overhead. This player is usually very athletic with quick reactions and good balance.

If you want to be a serve and volleyer, alter your service toss. The service toss should be slightly more in front of you than it would be for a normal serve, because you will be moving forward immediately after serving. Use the down-the-middle serve or the at-the-body serve, as those serves cut down on the angles that the returner may have. Hit the serve then take about three steps before executing the split step.

The volley hit immediately after the serve is one of the most important shots in a serve and volley game. It takes a lot of practice to feel confident with this shot. Against a good returner, you will be hitting it off your shoelaces. The most important thing about the first volley after the return is to be able to hit it deep so that you can set yourself up for a good volley.

The all-court player is very versatile and can play both the baseline and serve and volley game and will usually go with whatever is more advantageous according to the opponent, weather conditions, court surface, and so on. The all-court player will attack short balls with the approach shot and usually has a high level of conditioning.

The moonballer hits everything high and slow and rarely misses. The moonballer mostly uses high-bouncing lobs that are hit right back to the middle of the court. This is a low-risk style of play. A moonballer usually is extremely patient, extremely fit, and can run down anything and everything. Often, a moonballer's opponent will lose patience and start taking higher and higher risks, which only makes the moonballer happier.

Selecting a Strategy

The first question you should ask yourself when trying to figure out which strategy to use is, "What are my strengths and weaknesses?" Are you more confident in your ability to hit certain shots—serve, return of serve, forehand, backhand, volleys, overhead? What do you consider to be your strengths—speed, patience, or tenacity?

If you have reliable and aggressive ground strokes but are not confident at the net, you may want to use the baseliner game. Be sure to hit shots deep and look for good opportunities to hit more aggressive shots.

If you are playing against a baseliner, use the drop shot to make him or her go to the net, taking the baseliner out of his or her element. Another useful strategy is to hit lobs. Deep, high shots are hard to attack. This will frustrate the baseliner.

In order to be an effective serve and volleyer, you need a strong, accurate serve. You also need reliable, aggressive volleys and overheads. The serve and volley game is very aggressive and extremely athletic.

When playing against a serve and volleyer, hit the service return at the incoming player's shoes. This will force the serve and volleyer to volley up to you, giving you a good opportunity for a passing shot.

The all-court player needs to be confident at the baseline as well as at the net and should be able to adjust according to the opponent and other conditions, such as weather and court surface. The all-court player looks to attack the midcourt shot either with an approach shot to set up net shots or as an outright winner.

When playing against an all-court player, try hitting shots deep and high. An all-court player will want to attack any short shots, so keeping him or her well behind the baseline and waiting for your opportunity to attack should serve you well.

The moonballer has incredible patience and excellent lobs. The moonballer does not mind being out on the court for hours and will run everything down and hit a lob. Most of the time, the opponent will get frustrated and start making a lot of unforced errors by going for high-risk shots off high lobs. The moonballer usually does not want to go to the net and will play several feet behind the baseline in a defensive position.

There are two ways to counter a moonballer. First, find an opportunity to draw the moonballer to the net. This needs to be done carefully, as most shots the moonballer hits are not suitable for hitting drop shots off of (too high and deep). Wait for a ball that is not too high or too deep, hit a drop shot, and make the moonballer play the net. Second, hit a midcourt volley and attack. Instead of letting the moonballer's lobs bounce, wait for one that will not be too difficult to handle. Hit it as a volley approach shot and come into the net. The moonballer will most likely hit another lob. When he or she does, hit an overhead smash.

Other Tactical Situations

Use the weather and court conditions as part of your strategy planning. Playing indoors, where the sun and wind would not be a factor, is ideal for an attacking type of player (serve and volleyer, all-court, baseliner) because attacking requires precision. Without the sun and the wind, one may try to take more risks than when playing outdoors.

The sun can be a major factor in an outdoor match. When facing the sun, your opponent might not be able to be as aggressive on the serve as usual. Use this to your advantage and attack the serve. Another good tactic to use if your opponent is facing the sun is to use the lob frequently, maybe even get into the net for an aggressive and surprise attack after a good lob. If you are facing the sun and encounter a lob, it might be a better idea to let it bounce in order to lessen the degree of difficulty.

In windy conditions, take fewer risks than usual. Aim for the middle of the court rather than the deep corners. Use topspin to make the ball go high over the net but come down into the court.

When playing on grass, a serve and volley player may have an advantage because the serve and volleyer does not have to play the bounce. Bounces are less predictable and skid more on grass than on other surfaces. On clay courts, a baseliner may have the advantage, as clay tends to slow down the speed of play, neutralizing fast shots. The speed of hard courts falls between grass and clay tennis courts.

Give it a go

FIVE AND SHORT

This is a two-player, approach shot drill. This drill will help you practice getting into position to hit approach shots and close into the net for the volley. Both players start at the baseline. One player hits a ball into play. Hit five baseline rally shots, then hit the sixth one short, near the service line. The seventh shot should be an approach shot hit down the line. Close into the net after you've hit the approach shot and play the point out.

SERVE AND VOLLEY I

This drill can be done alone. In this drill, you will practice serving, moving forward, and executing the split step for the serve and volley. Assume the normal starting stance for a serve. Toss the ball farther out in front of you than normal. Before contact, your upper body should be leaning into the court. After contact, take three quick steps into the court, then execute a split step. You should be able to make it to about the service line. Repeat 12 times for both the deuce and ad sides.

SERVE AND VOLLEY II

This is a two-player drill. One player is the server, the other is the returner. The server uses the same procedures as in Serve and Volley I. The returner returns the serve, the server hits a volley, then the players play the point out. Repeat 12 times for both the deuce and ad sides, then switch roles.

MOONBALLER GAME

In this modified partner game, both players play an entire set as the moonballer. If a short or weak ball is hit, it may be attacked. A player who loses a point due to an unforced error loses two points. Play a regular set using standard scoring.

COUNTER MOONBALLER GAME

In this modified partner game, one player is the moonballer while the other player tries to apply the counter strategies (waiting for an opportunity to draw the moonballer into the net or taking a lob out of the air as a volley and following it in to the net). Switch roles after every two games until a set is won.

APPLY A STRATEGY

This is a two-player modified game. In this drill, each player selects a playing type (baseliner, serve and volleyer, all-court player, or moonballer). Play a set, trying to incorporate the particular style of play while also trying to counter your opponent's style of play.

Set Point

As you develop into a more complete player with sound technique, tactics will become an important part of your game. High-percentage tennis is an important part of any player's game. Your particular style of play should be based on your strengths and weaknesses, your confidence, and your opponent's strengths and weaknesses. Experiment with different styles to see what works best for you. This may change as you evolve as a player.

In the next chapter, we cover the doubles game. Doubles is a very exciting game, with quick points. The fact that you have a teammate on the court makes it possible for your team to run plays, as in other team sports.

CHAPTER

Doubles Tactics

Doubles is a dynamic and exciting game. It involves playing quick, aggressive points and taking good risks at the right time. In this way, the doubles game is very different from the singles game.

Before you begin playing doubles, you need to understand some important things about the game. First, you need to understand the role of each position on the court and the basic doubles formation. Next, we look at three other formations. Finally, we cover some strategies to help you and your doubles partner take the court by storm.

You will find that doubles can be a whole lot of fun. With teamwork as an integral element of the game, choosing a partner that can psyche you up when you need it or calm you down when you need to, and vice versa, is an important part of playing well and having fun.

Positions and Roles

In the doubles game, you have four players on the court: the server, the server's partner, the returner, and the returner's partner (figure 12.1). Each player has an important role to play in the successful execution of the point (table 12.1).

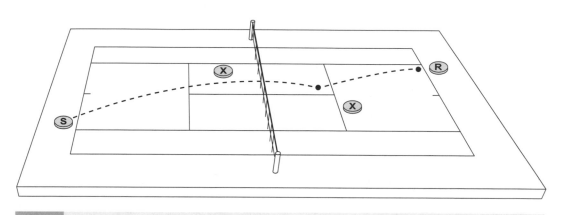

12.1 Doubles formation prior to serve.

Table 12.1

ROLES FOR DOUBLES PLAYERS				
Serving side			**Returning side**	
Player	**Role**		**Player**	**Role**
Server	Get a high percentage of first serves in Serve down the middle or to the returner's backhand		Returner	Get a high percentage of returns in Return crosscourt
Server's partner	Be aggressive Keep the feet moving Cut off any volleys within reach Poach		Returner's partner	Call the serve Act as a "goalie"

The Serving Side

The server stands behind the baseline midway between the center-mark and the singles sideline (figure 12.2). Because in the doubles game the alleys are in and the court is covered by two players, the server stands in a different place than he or she would if playing singles.

The server's most important job is to successfully complete a high percentage of first serves. The server's secondary job is to try to get the serve down the middle or to the returner's backhand. The down-the-middle serve is an important tool in the doubles game because it reduces the angles available to the returner, thereby making the server's partner more effective.

12.2   The server.

The server's partner (figure 12.3) should stand in the middle of the service box. The server's partner's job is to try to hit anything within reach. Remember that in doubles volleys are more desirable than ground strokes, so if you can hit a volley, hit it! A good target is the returner's partner's feet. Any shot hit at the feet is very tough to return.

Another important job for the server's partner is to keep the feet moving. Not only does this keep the server's partner active and ready for any shot, but it keeps the opponents aware of his or her presence.

12.3   **The server's partner.**

The Return Side

The returner (figure 12.4) stands in the basic return position near the baseline, inside the singles sideline. The returner's number one job is to get the return back and in. The returner's second job is to hit a crosscourt shot to keep the ball away from the server's partner.

12.4 **The returner.**

The returner's partner should stand at the service line, close to the center service line (figure 12.5). The returner's partner's first job is to call the serve, since he or she has the best view of the service line.

The returner's partner's second job is a little tougher. If the returner cannot get the return crosscourt far enough to avoid the server's partner, the returner's partner must try to hit the ball back in off the shoelaces. This is a tough shot but, with practice, it is a fun position to be in. I call this position the goalie because the returner's partner cannot let anything pass, just like a goalie in hockey.

Boundaries and Rotation

Doubles rules are similar to singles rules with a couple of exceptions. The boundaries are a bit different, as the alleys are inbounds for all shots in doubles except for the serve. The serve must still go in the service boxes, just as in singles.

In terms of service rotation, let's say players A and B are playing against C and D. Player A serves out the first game, followed by player C, then player B, then player D. That rotation (A, C, B, D) must be kept throughout the whole set. At the start of a new set, a doubles team can choose to change the order of serve if they want to.

When returning serve, you must always return serve from the same side (ad or deuce side) for the whole set. Again, at the start of a new set, you and your partner may decide to switch sides but you must return from that side for the entire set.

Doubles Formations

The one-up, one-back formation (figure 12.6) is the basic starting position of most doubles points. The back player's main job is to keep the ball in play, keep the ball away from the opposing player at the net (keep it crosscourt), and hit to the opponent's feet if they advance to the net. This formation develops before the ball is put into play. Often both the serving and returning sides are in one-up, one-back formations.

The up player's task is a bit more aggressive. Since this player is in the volley position, this player should attack whenever possible. Remember to keep your feet moving during the point so that you can pounce on a ball at any time.

Three other formations that can be used when playing doubles are the both-up formation, the Australian formation (also known as the I formation), and the both-back formation.

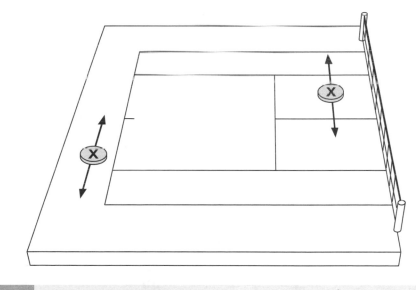

| 12.6 | One-up, one-back formation. |

In the both-up formation (figure 12.7), both players on the same team are at the net. It would be against the rules to start this way at the beginning of a point, but after the serve either the server or the returner is allowed to approach the net to join his or her partner. This is a formidable formation. For the opposing team, this wall will be very hard to penetrate.

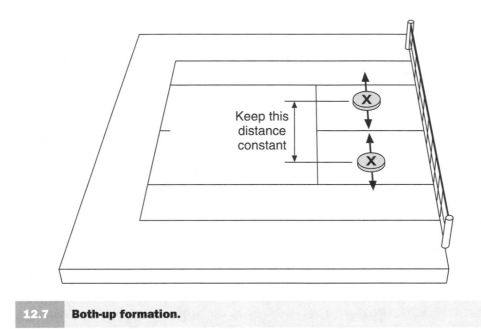

Keep this distance constant

12.7   **Both-up formation.**

If you and your partner have good volleys and overheads, your team should definitely practice the both-up formation. To make this an effective tactic, players must move together both side-to-side and up and back. For the side-to-side movements, remember two things: try to make the distance between you and your partner constant, and move together with the ball. This is called tracking. For example, if your partner moves a bit to the left because the ball is on the deuce side on the other side of the court, you should move a bit to the left as well. For up and back movements, try to stay even with each other and move forward when in an offensive situation. Move slightly back when in a defensive situation.

The Australian formation (or I formation) (figure 12.8) is used by the serving team at the start of a point. This is an aggressive formation. It puts a lot of pressure on the returner to get the return past the server's partner.

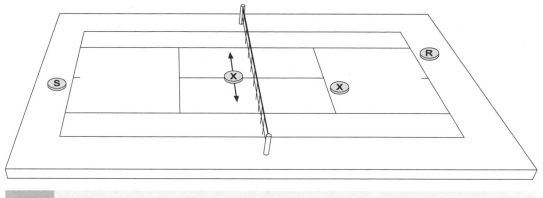

Australian formation (or I formation).

The server starts in the singles serving position. The server's partner has two options: start crouched at the center service line near
the net or start in a regular ready position across from the returner's
partner. After the serve is hit, the server's partner goes to either the
ad side or deuce side as preplanned by the serving team before the
serve is hit. The server then needs to cover the other side.

This formation is useful when your team has a good server. It puts
a tremendous amount of pressure on the returning team. It is an
excellent formation to use against a good crosscourt returner because it forces the returner to hit it down the line. It is also a useful
formation when you want to change it up a bit, give your opponents
a new look and something to think about.

The both-back formation (figure 12.9) can be used by the returning team. In this formation, both players on the returning team start
at the baseline. Although this formation is somewhat defensive, it
can come in handy at times. This formation is used when one or

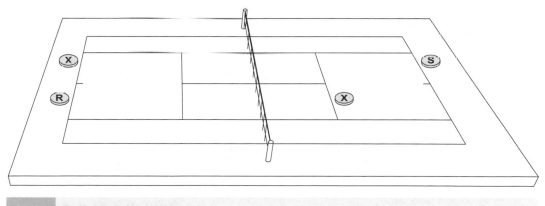

12.9   **Both-back formation.**

both returners are having difficulty keeping the return away from the server's partner. This may be because the serve is very strong or because the server's partner is very aggressive.

This formation takes some pressure away from the returner to keep it away from the server's partner. Usually when the ball is hit to the server's partner, that player has a fairly easy putaway shot. However, if the both-back formation is used by the returning team, they are in a better position to scramble and try to neutralize the point.

Doubles Strategies

These basic doubles-specific strategies are very important to successful doubles play at any level. Doubles strategies are slightly different from singles strategies. The most fundamental difference is that aggressiveness and gambling at the right times are very important in doubles, whereas in singles, consistency is key. Having a partner on the court with you also makes it easier to cover the court.

Communication

Communication during points is an important part of playing successful doubles. If a ball is between two players, one player should yell, "Mine!" so that both players know exactly what is going on. Short, one word commands work best when communicating on the court. You don't want both players going for the ball at the same time, or neither player going for the ball. This can happen on an overhead when both players are at the net or when both players are at the baseline for a ground stroke. It also can happen in a one-up, one-back situation when the ball comes down the middle. The worst that can happen in a doubles game is for the ball to go between both players as they look at each other, not knowing whether the other one is going to hit it or not.

Communication between points is just as important as communication during points. Studies have shown that teams that come together between points are more successful. Players who talk to each other, even if it is a simple "Here we go!" are more likely to play as a team than as two individuals. You do not have to solve the meaning of life when you come together between points. It is important, however, to check in with your partner and make sure he or she is okay. Sometimes one partner may think that the other is mad about a mistake, but in most cases that is not true at all! Not coming together between points only exacerbates such thoughts.

Poaching

Poaching (figure 12.10) is an aggressive move by the net person. The person at the net crosses to the other side of the court (deuce to ad or vice versa) to hit a volley. This usually happens after the serve off the return or in a one-up, one-back situation.

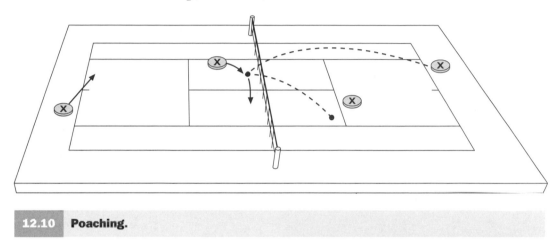

12.10   **Poaching.**

When the server's partner poaches off the return, the move is usually preplanned by the serving team. It can be preplanned verbally or with the use of hand signals. The server's partner determines whether to poach. If your team uses signals (figure 12.11), it is important to signal for every serve or else your opponents will catch on to the fact that you only signal when poaching.

When the server's partner shows an open hand, it means he or she is poaching. A closed fist means he or she is not poaching. An index finger indicates a fake. A well-timed fake will make the returner think you are going and might make the returner hit the ball down the line, which is a more difficult shot. Even if the returner manages to hit it, you are there for the volley.

12.11   **Hand signals can be used to indicate poaching.**

When poaching during a point, the net person will cross and hit a volley off a regular ground stroke. This usually happens when the two baseline people are engaged in a crosscourt rally. When the net person poaches in any situation, it is important for the net person's partner to cover the other side.

Switching

Switching (figure 12.12) occurs when at least one person is at the net, a lob is hit over the net person's head, and the net person cannot hit an overhead off it. Instead of the net player running back and trying to hit the ball, the partner should take responsibility for the ball by moving over while the net person switches to the other side. If both players are already at the net, the player who is not on the ball side must run diagonally to the ball while the net person switches to the other side. Quick and loud communication is an important part of switching. As soon as a player realizes the situation at hand, she or he should yell, "Switch!"

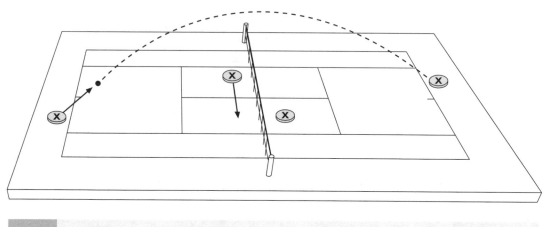

12.12 **Switching.**

Aim for the Feet

Hitting at your opponent's feet is a valuable weapon in doubles. Not only is it extremely difficult for your opponent to get the shot back to you, but even if they do hit it back, they need to hit the ball up to you. Whenever you encounter a shot that you cannot attack, hitting at your opponent's feet is the next choice.

PLAY!

Go out and play some doubles. The best way to learn doubles is to play. Make sure that you know where to position yourself for each position. Also make sure that you rotate correctly between points.

POACHING I

This drill requires a coach or feeder and three or more players. The feeder should have a basket of balls and stand in the return of serve position (figure 12.13). Players should line up at the server's partner position, straight across from the feeder. The feeder hits a crosscourt shot out of hand. The first player in line runs across and poaches (hits a volley) off the feed. The first player continues across the court and then circles around to rejoin the line. The next person in line should be ready to go. After each player hits 10 shots, switch sides.

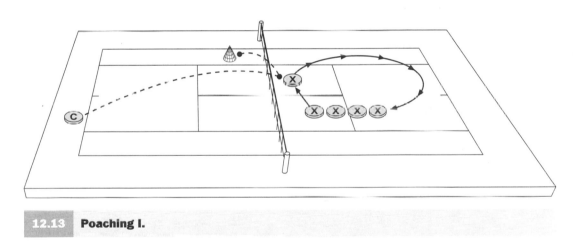

12.13 Poaching I.

POACHING II

This drill is a modified version of poaching drill I. At least six players are needed. Four players assume the four positions on the doubles court (server, server's partner, returner, and returner's partner). The other two players wait behind the server's side of the court. The server hits an underhand ball into the service box (figure 12.14). The returner returns it crosscourt, while the server's partner poaches. The server covers the other side of the court. Play the point out. As soon as the point ends, the server becomes the server's partner, the next person in line becomes the server, and the server's partner joins the end of the line. The returning side does not rotate. Play to seven points, then switch sides so the returning players are on the poaching side and vice versa.

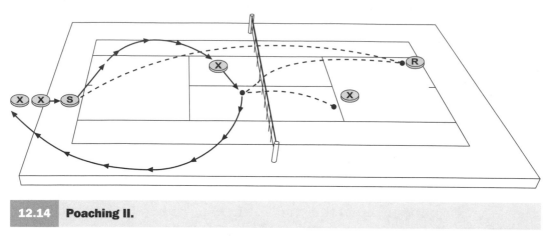

12.14 **Poaching II.**

SWITCH DRILL

Four or more players are needed for this drill. The switch is emphasized. Start with the four players in doubles positions; any extra players wait at the back of the court. The returner starts the point with a high, deep lob over the server's partner. The server's partner calls out, "Mine!" or "Switch!" If the server's partner says, "Mine!", he or she hits the overhead. If the server's partner yells, "Switch!", the server must run over and hit the ball as both players switch positions. Play the point out. Play two points, then rotate in one big circle as shown in figure 12.15.

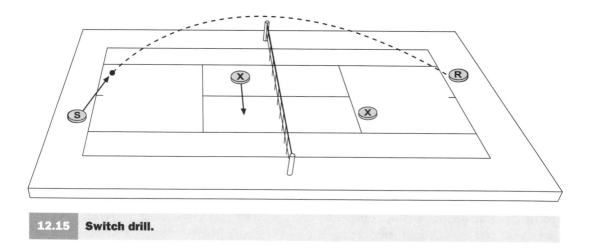

12.15 **Switch drill.**

SERVE AND RETURN CROSSCOURT GAME

Two players can play this game. One player starts as the server, the other as the returner. Points are played out on the diagonal doubles court as shown in figure 12.16. Anything not in the diagonal court is out. Players may elect to come into the net or stay back. Play each game to seven points, making sure that both players get to serve from both sides.

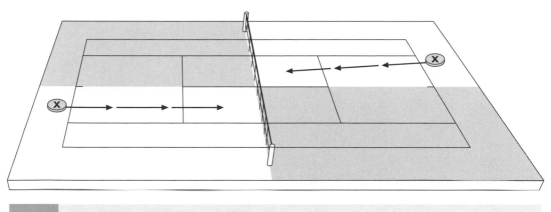

12.16 Serve and return crosscourt game.

MODIFIED DOUBLES

You will need two doubles teams to play modified doubles. Start a set as if playing a normal doubles game. Anytime a team wins the point off a volley or an overhead, two points are awarded. This puts emphasis on net play.

Game, Set, and Match

Doubles is an exciting game. Having four people on the court, as opposed to just two for the singles game, greatly changes the dynamics on the court. As you practice the skills outlined in this chapter, you will become a more complete doubles player.

I hope you've enjoyed this introduction to tennis. Tennis is a great sport not only because it's challenging and provides great exercise, but it is also a lifelong sport. Seeing improvement in the consistency of your ground strokes, adding more pace to your volleys, or developing a kick serve can provide immense satisfaction. Tennis also gives you the opportunity to interact with other tennis players at an intense but fun level. Practice hard and have fun playing!

About the Writer

Carol Matsuzaki is an assistant professor of physical education at the Massachusetts Institute of Technology, where she teaches beginning through advanced tennis classes. Since taking over as head coach of the women's tennis team in the spring of 1998, Matsuzaki has led her team to four consecutive Newmac Conference titles (1999-2002). She was named Newmac Conference Women's Tennis Coach of the Year in 1999, 2000, and 2001.

Sports Fundamentals Series

Learning sports basics has never been more effective—or more fun—than with the new Sports Fundamentals Series. These books enable recreational athletes to engage in the activity quickly. Quick participation, not hours of reading, makes learning more fun and more effective.

Each chapter addresses a specific skill for that particular sport, leading the athlete through a simple, four-step sequence:

- *You Can Do It:* The skill is introduced with sequential instructions and accompanying photographs.

- *More to Choose and Use:* Variations and extensions of the primary skill are covered.

- *Take It to the Court/Field:* Readers learn how to apply the skill in competition.

- *Give It a Go:* These provide several direct experiences for gauging, developing, and honing the skill.

The writers of the Sports Fundamentals Series books are veteran instructors and coaches with extensive knowledge of their sport. They make learning and playing the sport more enjoyable for readers. And because the series covers a wide selection of sports, you can get up to speed quickly on any sport you want to play.

In addition to Tennis, the Sports Fundamentals Series will include:

• Soccer	• Basketball	• Golf	• Softball	• Weight Training
• Archery	• Bowling	• Volleyball	• Racquetball	

HUMAN KINETICS
The Premier Publisher for Sports & Fitness
P.O. Box 5076, Champaign, IL 61825-5076
www.HumanKinetics.com

2335

To place your order, U.S. customers call
TOLL FREE 800-747-4457
Canada 800-465-7301
Australia (08) 8277 1555
New Zealand 0064 9 448 1207
Europe +44 (0) 113 255 5665

*You'll find
other outstanding
tennis resources at*

www.HumanKinetics.com

In the U.S. call

1-800-747-4457

Australia.............................. 08 8277 1555
Canada 1-800-465-7301
Europe......................+44 (0) 113 255 5665
New Zealand................... 0064 9 448 1207

HUMAN KINETICS
The Premier Publisher for Sports & Fitness
P.O. Box 5076 • Champaign, IL 61825-5076 USA